VISUALIZING ABSTRACT
OBJECTS AND RELATIONS

——————A Constraint-Based Approach——————

World Scientific Series in Computer Science*

*To view the complete list of the published volumes in the series, please visit:
http://www.worldscientific.com/series/wsscs

Series in Computer Science — Vol. 5

VISUALIZING ABSTRACT OBJECTS AND RELATIONS

—————A Constraint-Based Approach—————

Tomihisa Kamada

World Scientific
Singapore • New Jersey • London • Hong Kong

Published by

World Scientific Publishing Co. Pte. Ltd.

5 Toh Tuck Link, Singapore 596224

USA office: 27 Warren Street, Suite 401-402, Hackensack, NJ 07601

UK office: 57 Shelton Street, Covent Garden, London WC2H 9HE

British Library Cataloguing-in-Publication Data
A catalogue record for this book is available from the British Library.

World Scientific Series in Computer Science — Vol. 5
VISUALIZING ABSTRACT OBJECTS AND RELATIONS

ISBN-13 978-981-02-0009-1
ISBN-10 981-02-0009-9

To my father and mother

PREFACE

Pictorial representations are very useful for human to understand complicated relations and structures. This is the reason that visualization of information handled in computers is becoming more and more important in the communication between human and computer. The user interface of information systems is strongly required to visualize many kinds of information in a wide variety of graphical forms. At present, however, only some very specialized visualization techniques have been developed probably because the generality in visualization has not been appreciated correctly. The goal of this book is to present a general visualization framework for translating abstract objects and relations, typically represented in textual forms, into pictorial representations. We have implemented a visualization system based on this framework, and show the successful results.

In our framework, abstract objects and relations are mapped to graphical objects and relations by user-defined mapping rules. The declarative, nature of our mapping rules provides users with more global and more flexible layout capability. The kernel of our visualization process is to determine a layout of graphical objects under geometric constraints. A constraint-based object layout system named COOL has been developed to handle this layout problem. COOL introduces the concept of rigidity of constraints in order to reasonably handle a set of conflicting constraints by the use of the least square method.

We also present an algorithm for drawing general undirected graphs in order to visualize network structures as network diagrams. The algorithm has many good properties such as symmetric drawings of symmetric graphs, almost congruent drawings of isomorphic graphs, uniform distribution of vertices, and a relatively small number of edge crossings. In addition, it is applied to radial drawings in which vertices are placed on concentric circles and to layered drawings in which vertices are placed on parallel lines.

The proposed visualization framework is shown to be general enough to be applied to various types of visualization problems, such as the visualization of semantics of natural language sentences, the generation of diagrams for data structures and for program structures, and the drawing of database schema. The examples of all these problems are shown with the actual mapping rules and the pictorial results.

This book is based on the dissertation which the author submitted to the University of Tokyo for the degree of DSc in Information Science. We believe that many researchers and students who work on computer science, especially on data visualization, user interface, constraint-based systems, and automatic graph drawing, will have interest in this book.

ACKNOWLEDGEMENTS

I could complete the work presented here thanks to a lot of people who have helped me in some ways. First I would like to express my highest gratitude to Professor Satoru Kawai who was my supervisor while I was a graduate student at the University of Tokyo. He has continuously supported and encouraged me. His valuable comments and suggestions have really improved this work. I am also grateful to those who were or are the members of Kawai Laboratory for helpful discussions with them. They are Tamiya Onodera, Hiroshi Morishima, Chien Lee, Satoshi Matsuoka, and Ken Nakayama. Special thanks to Satoshi Matsuoka for his effort to improve the computing environment of our laboratory.

I would like to thank Peter Eades (University of Queensland, Australia) for his valuable comments on our graph drawing algorithm. He also informed me of many related work. Discussions with him on automatic graph drawing were very useful.

Since this work is related to various research areas, discussions with many people in different research areas have greatly helped me. I have discussed the problems in drawing graphs and our drawing algorithm with Katsuhiro Ota who studies graph theory. Shuichi Moritsugu told me about the recent progress of symbolic manipulation systems. I am indebted to Nobuo Satake for his program for parsing English sentences, which I used to realize the applications of our system. I have been also stimulated by those whom I have talked with at public research meetings. In addition, I am thankful to many researchers who sent me their papers.

On the personal side, I would like to thank my parents, brother and sister for their support and encouragement. Finally a thousand thanks to my close friends who made the time enjoyable.

CONTENTS

VISUALIZING ABSTRACT OBJECTS AND RELATIONS

———A Constraint-Based Approach———

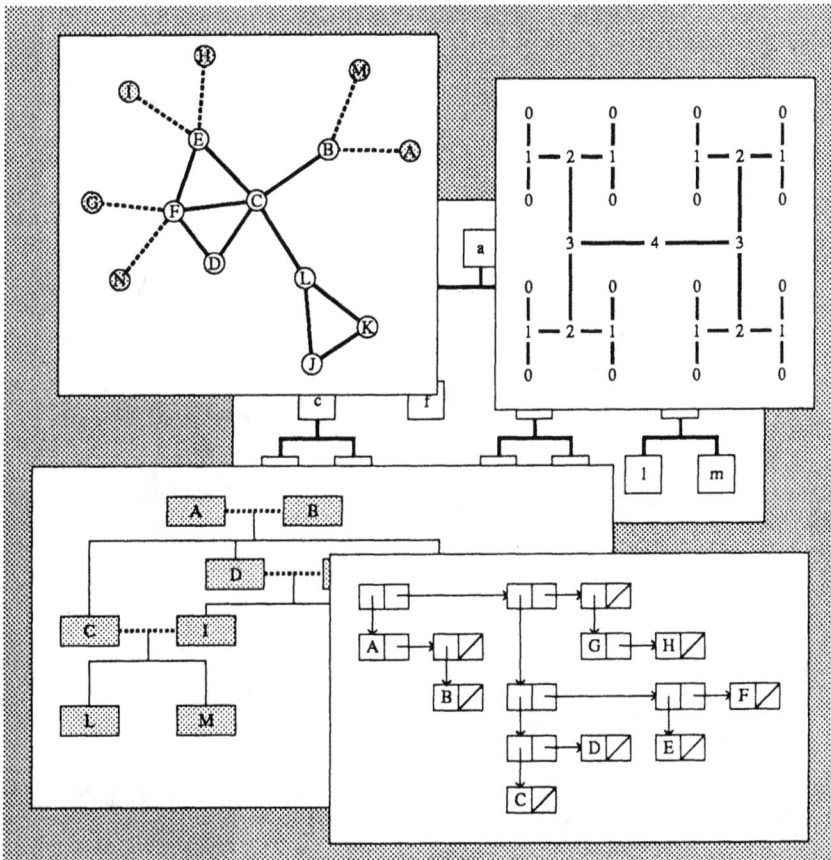

CHAPTER 1

INTRODUCTION

As it has been said that a picture is worth a thousand words, pictorial representations of information have been playing an important role in human communication and recognition since time immemorial. Human can grasp the content of a picture much faster than he can scan and understand a text sentence, because he has the ability to recognize the spatial configuration of elements in a picture and notice the relationships between elements quickly. Visual communication is today also indispensable for the interface between human and computer. Recent rapid progress of technology of high-performance workstations and personal computers with high-resolution bit-map displays has opened a new age of visual human-computer interactions. The user interface of information systems is strongly required to visualize many kinds of information in a wide variety of graphical forms. This book describes research on the visualization of information handled in information systems, which is a fundamental problem of visual communication.

Usually it costs much to implement a graphical presentation module (program) because a "good" pictorial representation heavily depends both on the data handled in information systems and on the purpose of presentation. It would be, therefore, considered challenging to realize general tools for data visualization. As for numeric data, the visualization problem has been studied intensively, and the tools called business graph packages have already spread widely. Recently visualization in scientific computing is also studied by many researchers. However, a general technique for visualizing abstract objects and relations has not yet been developed. We present a framework for translating textual representations of (currently static) abstract objects and relations into pictorial representations, and describe a general platform for visualization.

1.1. Motivation

Computer graphics technology has grown rapidly since Sutherland proved that an interactive graphical interface was an effective way for man-machine communication in the early 1960s [126]. At present, researches on computer graphics branch off in various directions. It is one direction to create realistic images of 3D objects by using the techniques of ray-tracing and advanced reflectance models. We have been more interested in another direction of generating illustrative pictures. We have already presented the research on advanced graphics for visualization of shielding relations among 3D objects [62, 64]. In the research, we have proposed the scheme (Picturing Function scheme) in which the attributes of subparts of primitives are determined depending on the shielding environment. Each hidden part of a primitive is characterized by such and such primitives which hide it, and the attribute of the part is determined from this shielding relation by the user-defined procedure. In an experimental system named GRIP which implemented this scheme, a variety of shielding relations are visualized as drawing styles and colors.

In our view, it is one of the most important applications of graphics to represent non-graphical relations graphically. The above research is one example. Business graphics is also a typical example of visualizing non-graphical relations. In business graphics systems, numeric or quantitative relational information is visualized as a variety of graphical forms: for example, bar charts, pie charts, line graphs, scatter plots, and Chernoff's face plots. In these charts, quantitative relations are represented as sizes, areas, positions, shapes, and colors of graphical objects. To draw diagrams for representing complicated structures is of course another example. Many kinds of information is required to be visualized so that viewers can understand the underlying structures easily. Our concern is how to visualize complicated relational structures systematically by computers.

However, currently available graphics tools have not yet reached high-level interfaces enough to visualize complicated relational structures easily. When a user wants to represent data of a specific format in a specific graphical format, he must make a program for reading the data and drawing the pictures he wants by using a graphics library or a standard graphics package.[1] Existing graphics languages and systems do not help us translate original abstract relations into pictorial representations systematically, because they only provide drawing instructions. This situation can be said quite bad for software production and maintenance. The total visualization process beyond a mere graphics system should be studied. The goal of our research is to fill up this gap between applications and graphics systems and to pioneer a new research area of visualization of abstract objects and relations.

1.2. Visualizing Abstract Objects and Relations

A set of pictures (diagrams) can be viewed as a language in the sense that picture elements (graphical objects) such as boxes, circles, and text strings are arranged under certain rules. Therefore the visualization process can be regarded as the translation from textual languages into two- or three-

---

[1] For example, GKS (Graphical Kernel System) [45] and PHIGS (Programmer's Hierarchical Interactive Graphics System) [4] are available.

dimensional visual languages. We call this process "translation into pictures." Textual data represented by certain syntactic rules has a semantic interpretation. What should be visualized is this semantic or relational structure. In our approach, a relational structure (in other words, a semantic network) is regarded as a set of abstract relations among abstract objects. An essential criterion for good pictures is whether human can find the layout rules in the pictures intuitively and understand the underlying structures easily. Our idea for visualization is derived from this fact. That is, we generate a picture by mapping a relational structure to simple layout rules (such as horizontal and vertical listings) and explicit line connections. This mapping, which we call "visual mapping," is controlled by users.[2]

The translation process works as follows. First the data represented by the syntax of each application is translated into the relational structure representation of abstract objects and relations. Secondly abstract objects are mapped to graphical objects, and abstract relations among them are mapped to graphical relations among the corresponding graphical objects. Graphical relations treated here are geometric relations, connectional relations, and attribute relations. Finally an actual layout of graphical objects is computed by solving graphical constraints, and then a picture is generated. In order to handle this layout problem, we have developed a layout system named COOL (COnstraint-based Object Layout system). COOL can handle over-constrained cases which have been treated as errors by existing constraint-based graphics systems. In COOL, over-constrained equation systems are solved approximately by the least square method.

We must take into account the cases in which network structures are desired to be visualized as network diagrams literally. As a special visual mapping, a technique for visualizing network structures generally is

---

[2] The picturing function in GRIP [62, 64] can be regarded as a visual mapping in a wide sense, though it handles geometric objects instead of abstract objects. The picturing function maps shielding relations among geometric objects to drawing attributes.

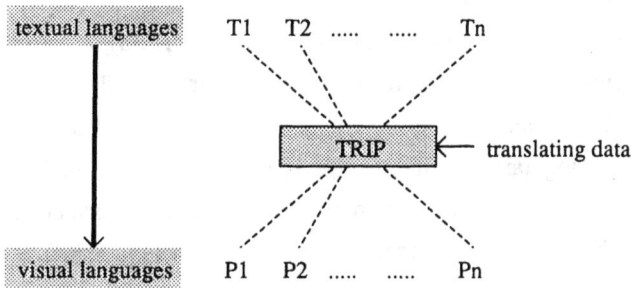

Figure 1.1: TRIP, a general platform for visualization.

incorporated into our scheme.[3] In order to realize this, we have developed an algorithm for drawing general undirected graphs [66]. In this algorithm, every two objects, whether they are adjacent or not, are constrained to keep certain Euclidean distance. These constraints are solved approximately by the least square method. Thus this mapping is also designed on the principle of finding out a compromise under conflicting constraints. The least square approximation is a powerful way to deal with conflicting constraints induced when multi-dimensional relations are to be represented in a two-dimensional restricted space.

We have realized a visualization system named TRIP (TRanslation Into Pictures) as a prototype based on our visualization framework. TRIP is independent both of input textual languages and of output visual languages as Figure 1.1 illustrates. In order to clear the purpose of our system, we show a snapshot of its applications which will appear in Chapter 6. Five

---

[3] Displaying general views of various data handled in information systems besides network structures is necessary for the construction of good user interfaces. We have already handled and proposed a method for displaying general pictures of three-dimensional objects [65].

examples of translation which are actually performed by TRIP are illustrated
in Figure 1.2. The input textual representation and the output pictorial
representation are shown in each example. In Fig. 1.2(a), a set of English
sentences representing a graphical layout is translated into a picture
representing the corresponding layout. In Fig. 1.2(b), a set of English sentences representing family relationships is translated into a pedigree chart.
In Fig. 1.2(c), a list data written in LISP notation is translated into a list
diagram in which cells are connected by arrows. In Fig. 1.2(d), a piece of
program written in C language is translated into a structured diagram called
a Nassi-Shneiderman diagram. In Fig. 1.2(e), an entity-relationship (ER)
schema written in Prolog is translated into an entity-relationship diagram.
We treat these translation processes based on the same framework, although
they may look apparently quite different. As these examples show, a wide
range of visualization problems can be handled in our system.

TRIP provides users with many kinds of primitive graphical relations.
It is the users' responsibility how to use these relations in specifying the
visual mapping data. However, some people may claim that it is difficult to
choose the most suitable visual mapping for their data and purposes. In fact,
it is not an easy question what is a good pictorial representation (visual
metaphor). This problem is closely related to human cognition, and we will
not discuss it in this book. Our purpose is to build a general and convenient
platform whose users can get desired presentation systems by specifying the
visual mapping data. The results in cognitive science on human interface
will be taken into the visual mapping.

1.3. Contributions of the Work

There are three primary contributions of this research. The first one is a
framework for visualizing abstract objects and relations. The second one is
the COOL system into which several new ideas are introduced. COOL
plays an important role in realization of our visualization framework, and
can be also used separately as a high-level graphics system. In fact, all the

CONNECT is a large white circle.
AGENT, OBJECT, GOAL, and STYLE are large boxes.
AGENT, OBJECT, and GOAL are arranged horizontally.
CONNECT is put above AGENT, OBJECT, and GOAL with connecting lines.
STYLE is put on the right of CONNECT with a connecting line.
BOX1, BOX2, and BOX3 are small white circles.
LINE, AND, TO, and SOLID are also small white circles.
LINE is put below AGENT with a thick dashed line.
PROPERTIES is a large box.
PROPERTIES is put below LINE with a line.
SOLID lies below PROPERTIES.
SOLID is connected by a thick dashed line to PROPERTIES.
OBJECT is put above BOX1 with a thick dashed line.
GOAL is put above TO with a thick dashed line.
AND is placed below TO.
BOX2 and BOX3 lie below AND.
AND is connected to BOX2, BOX3, and TO by lines.
BOX2 is laid on the left of BOX3.
PRESENT and PASSIVE are white standard boxes.
PRESENT is put on the right of STYLE with a dotted line.
PASSIVE is placed under PRESENT.
PASSIVE is also connected to STYLE by a dotted line.

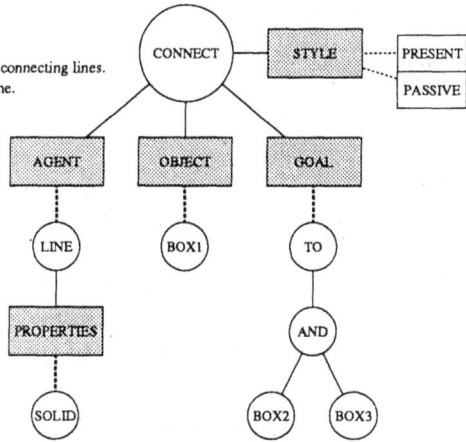

(a) English sentences → a graphical layout

B is the wife of A.
C, D, E are the children of A.
D is the husband of H.
I and J are the children of H.
E is the father of G.
F is the mother of G.
K is the child of J.
G is the mother of K.
L and M are the children of C.
C is the husband of I.

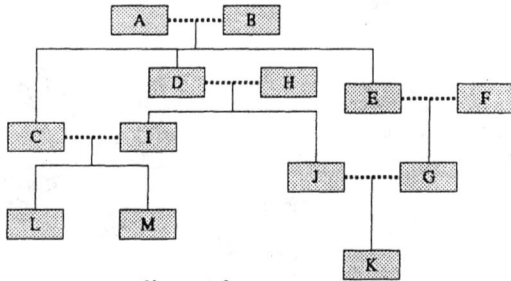

(b) English sentences → a pedigree chart

((A(B))(((C)D)(E)F)(GH))

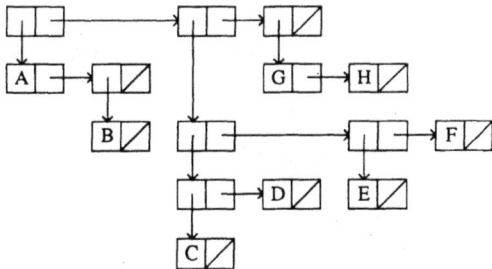

(c) an S-expression → a list diagram

Figure 1.2:   Visualization by TRIP.

```
int binarysearch(int x, int v[], int n)
{
int low, high, mid;
low = 0;
high = n - 1;
while (low <= high) {
mid = (low + high) / 2;
if (x < v[mid])
high = mid - 1;
else if(x > v[mid])
low = mid + 1;
else
return mid;
}
return -1;
}
```

int binarysearch(int x, int v[], int n)			
int low, high, mid;			
low = 0;			
high = n - 1;			
while (low <= high)			
	mid = (low + high) / 2;		
	T x < v[mid] F		
	high = mid - 1;	T x > v[mid] F	
		low = mid + 1;	return mid;
return -1;			

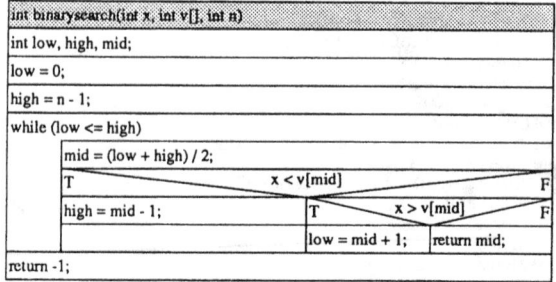

(d) a program text → a Nassi-Shneiderman diagram

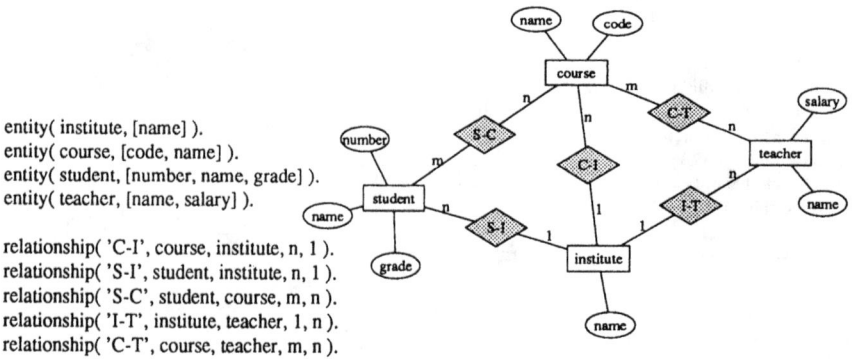

```
entity( institute, [name] ).
entity( course, [code, name] ).
entity( student, [number, name, grade] ).
entity( teacher, [name, salary] ).

relationship( 'C-I', course, institute, n, 1 ).
relationship( 'S-I', student, institute, n, 1 ).
relationship( 'S-C', student, course, m, n ).
relationship( 'I-T', institute, teacher, 1, n ).
relationship( 'C-T', course, teacher, m, n ).
```

(e) an ER schema → an ER diagram

Figure 1.2: Visualization by TRIP (continued).

illustrations in this book were generated by COOL. The last one is a new algorithm for drawing general undirected graphs, which can be used for displaying general views of network structures. A secondary contribution is the visualization of semantics of natural language sentences, which is realized as an application of our system. In this application, the semantic relations derived from English sentences are mapped to the graphical relations.

The rest of this section describes the primary contributions of this research in more detail.

(1) A general framework for visualizing abstract objects and relations.

We present a general visualization framework in which abstract objects and abstract relations are visualized as graphical objects (such as boxes and circles) and graphical relations (such as horizontal/vertical listings and line connections) among graphical objects according to user-defined translation rules. In our framework, a visualization problem results in a constrained layout problem of graphical objects. The whole mechanism for translating arbitrary textual representations into desired pictorial representations is presented.

(2) A constraint-based object layout system.

We present a constraint-based object layout system (COOL) which is designed to compute a layout automatically from the specification of geometric relations among graphical objects. COOL introduces the classification of constraints (rigid constraints and pliable constraints) and the least square constraint satisfaction by which conflicting constraints can be solved approximately. A graphical layout can be specified structurally by the picture hierarchy mechanism. In this case, the system solves constraints hierarchically by traversing the picture hierarchy. These techniques enable us to cope with complicated layout problems encountered in practical use.

(3) An algorithm for drawing general undirected graphs.

The basic idea of this algorithm follows. The desirable "geometric" distance between every two vertices in the drawing is regarded as the "graph theoretic" distance between them in the graph. By our algorithm, symmetric graphs are drawn as symmetric pictures, and isomorphic graphs are mostly drawn as the same picture(s). Our algorithm can also draw weighted graphs in the same way by relating weights to distances in the drawing. In addition, it can be applied to radial drawings in which vertices are placed on concentric circles and to layered drawings in which vertices are placed on parallel lines.

1.4. Organization of the Book

The remainder of this book is organized as follows. In the next chapter, we survey the existing work related to our research. Our research has relations with various areas in computer science, and in fact many literatures in different areas are referred to throughout this book.

In Chapter 3, we present a general visualization framework. We discuss the visualization process as the translation from textual representations into pictorial representations. The visual mapping which takes a central role in this translation is described.

In Chapter 4, we describe the COOL system in detail. First we explain the picture generation specification in COOL by giving examples, and then we describe the advanced features such as pliable constraints and the picture hierarchy mechanism. The constraint satisfaction mechanism is also presented. If you are only interested in constraint-based graphics or layout systems, read this chapter.

In Chapter 5, we present an algorithm for drawing general undirected graphs in detail. We show a lot of resultant pictures generated by the use of the algorithm. The extended versions of the algorithm for radial drawings and for layered drawings are also described. If you want to know only our graph drawing algorithm, you can understand it by reading this chapter separately.

In Chapter 6, we describe five practical applications of TRIP whose snapshot we have shown above. In each example, the actual visual mappings and the pictorial results are shown.

In Chapter 7, we propose the inverse translation based on our visualization framework. We apply it to direct manipulation systems and the general image recognition problem.

Finally we conclude in Chapter 8 by describing the future work and the long-term goals of our research.

CHAPTER 2

RELATED WORK

This chapter surveys a large range of existing work related to our research. Though the study of visualizing information has a long history, a general approach to the visualization problems is not yet explored. No study has directly influenced our whole work. However, some aspects of our research are related to previous and current work in various research areas. We categorize the related work into the following three areas: information presentation, high-level graphics systems and languages, and automatic graph drawing. Information presentation problems have been studied separately in different areas. We can find these work in business graphics, scientific visualization, database systems, visual languages,[1] algorithm animation, and so on. Existing high-level graphics systems and languages

---

[1] The term visual language is used for several meanings. Chang classifies visual languages into four types: languages that support visual interactions, visual programming languages, visual information processing languages, and iconic visual information processing languages [28, 29]. In this book, the term is used for visual programming languages or merely for graphical representations of logical structures.

including constraint-based ones have influenced the design of COOL. In the
area of automatic graph drawing, various algorithms for drawing several
classes of graphs are studied. A new algorithm for drawing general
undirected graphs which we propose here brings a significant result in this
area.

2.1. Information Presentation

Information processed in computers is so various that information
presentation problems have been studied in domain-dependent ways. There
have been a lot of studies on the visualization of specific information. As
for numeric data, many systems which automate business graphs and statistical graphs are developed [26, 48, 115]. In [131], an interactive system
which allows users to produce Cartesian plots, histograms, network
diagrams, and pie charts is presented. Mackinlay presents research on
automating the design of effective graphical presentations (such as bar
charts, scatter plots, and connected graphs) of relational information [83].
Scientific visualization which enables scientists to observe their simulations
and computations is a hot topic in computer graphics [91].

AIPS [145] is a knowledge-based information presentation system
implemented as a KLONE taxonomic hierarchy of display structure descriptions. In [6], a system for constructing user interface displays is built on
knowledge representation systems. In order to realize a general presentation
system which covers a wide range of presentation variations, it is important
to build a knowledge-base of presentation information like these systems.
The presentation database supporting a large repertoire of pictorial formats
can be built on our system.

Database systems use Bachman diagrams or entity-relationship
diagrams to show the structures of databases graphically [133, 135]. There
is some work on drawing these diagrams automatically [128, 141]. A graphical browser for entity-relationship database is presented in [25]. However,
the browser supports only a few presentation formats of schema graphs,

such as mandala format and rectangular format.

Pictures have been also used in programming since the birth of computers. The study of visualizing programs began with drawing flowcharts by computers [70]. The utility of flowcharts in programming was investigated [118], and many improved diagrams such as Nassi-Shneiderman diagrams [97], Chapin charts [30], Ferstl charts [46], and PAD (Problem Analysis Diagram) [49, 85] have been developed. State diagrams (graphs) have been used for the concise representation of the behavior of automata. Data flow diagrams show the flows of data clearly. We often use Petri nets to show low-level control flows. On displaying data structures, several studies have been done. For example, the Incense system [95] generates pictures for any data type during the execution of a program.

Recent advance of interactive graphics has encouraged the programming in graphical environments. Such a new programming technique is called visual or graphical programming. The existing work in this area is surveyed in [28, 55, 106, 119]. A variety of techniques for visualizing control flows and data structures are developed. Algorithm animation is also related to the visualization. Several systems for illustrating the behavior of algorithms are developed [14, 22, 23]. The design of information presentation is an important function of UIMSs (User Interface Management Systems). Peridot [96] and Coral [127] should be noted as the systems introducing constraints. They present a promising direction of UIMSs.

There is another system which deserves to be mentioned. GRAFLOG is an experimental interactive graphics interface in which drawings receive linguistic interpretations [100-102]. In GRAFLOG, graphical structures are mapped to logical structures by the translation function. On this point, we can find a resemblance between TRIP and GRAFLOG. However GRAF-LOG is, if anything, a kind of visual language, and does not include the notion of constraints and the layout facilities.

The above information presentation problems belong to the application domain of our system TRIP. We will handle the problems of generating list diagrams, Nassi-Shneiderman diagrams, and entity-relationship diagrams in Chapter 6.

2.2. High-Level Graphics Languages and Systems

Our research involves the design of a high-level graphical layout system. We have designed COOL which uses constraints to specify the relationships among picture elements. The use of constraints in computer graphics is not a new idea. More than 20 years ago, Sutherland's Sketchpad [126] pioneered the use of constraints in graphics systems. It also provided an interactive graphical interface, and its users could construct a drawing by defining geometric constraints interactively. Borning's ThingLab [17-19] is a well-known graphical simulation laboratory based on constraints like Sketchpad. ThingLab is written in the Smalltalk-80 [53], and uses object-oriented techniques for constraint representation and satisfaction. GROW [7] is a similar object-oriented system for building graphical user interfaces. However, the form of constraints in GROW is restricted to acyclic dependencies. ThingLab is extended to animation (Animus) by introducing temporal constraints [38]. Sketchpad and ThingLab employ the constraint satisfaction techniques based on relaxation.[2] Steele's CONSTRAINTS [125] pioneered another type of constraint systems which use symbolic techniques for solving constraints.

Knuth's METAFONT [73] uses linear equations among the variables representing x- and y-coordinates of points in the design of character shapes. Van Wyk's IDEAL [137] is a language for typesetting graphics which can solve "slightly non-linear" equation systems.[3] The constraint solver of

---

[2] Relaxation is a classical numerical approximation method for iteratively finding solutions. The process of estimating the error and guessing new values is iterated until the error is minimized.

[3] Van Wyk says in [137] that a system of equations is slightly non-linear if there is an order in which the equations can be processed such that, after substituting results known from previous processing, the equation looks linear. For example, the simultaneous quadratic equations for finding the circle going through three points can be reduced to this form.

IDEAL [36] attempts to reduce a set of constraints to a linear system based on Gaussian elimination. Kernighan's PIC [68] is another concise language for typesetting graphics, in which users can specify the positions of graphical objects by referring to the previous objects. As the preprocessors of PIC, many programs for producing special-purpose diagrams are developed: for example, GRAP [13] for specialized graphs like dot charts and scatter plots and CHEM [12] for chemical diagrams.

Gosling's Magritte [54] is an interactive graphical layout system whose constraint satisfaction mechanism is based on the algebraic transformation of sets of constraints. Nelson's Juno [98] is a system which integrates a constraint-based language with a WYSIWYG (what-you-see-is-what-you-get) image editor. Juno uses Newton-Raphson iteration for solving constraints. Leler's Bertland [80] is a general-purpose constraint language based on augmented term rewriting. It is applied to computer-aided design [79].

TK!Solver [74] is a commercially available system for the IBM-PC which uses constraints for general-purpose problem solving. Constraints are solved directly by local propagation if possible, and otherwise by relaxation. Users of TK!Solver can manipulate mathematical models in a window-based direct dialogue. It should be noted that the idea of constraints is introduced into spreadsheet systems like VisiCalc and its descendents. In these systems, complicated dependencies among spreadsheet items are maintained, and the changes are automatically propagated.

Our layout system is also related to the symbolic layout in VLSI design. Some constraint-based layout systems [90, 111] are developed. In this area, a constraint refers to establishing a geometric relationship among the attributes of layout elements such as cells and wires. In order to solve a great number of constraints in VLSI layouts, Mata presents an efficient algorithm for solving equation systems of the form $x_i - x_j \geq d$ $(d > 0)$ and $x_i - x_j = e$ $(e > 0)$ [89].

Recently constraint solving is introduced into traditional logic programming languages [33, 78, 113]. Researchers in this area are trying to integrate various constraint solvers into logic programming. As this trend shows, constraint-based programming is believed to become a new programming paradigm.

2.3. Automatic Graph Drawing

Information structures can be viewed as graphs in the abstract. Basic algorithms for drawing graphs pleasingly are required in many fields of computer science. We are particularly interested in drawing general undirected graphs. The state of the art in automatic graph drawing is surveyed comprehensively in [44, 129]. Actually a lot of drawing algorithms have been developed so far. These algorithms are categorized according to their target classes of graphs such as trees, planar graphs, acyclic digraphs, and general graphs. Here we review briefly the existing work in these categories.

Concerning trees, the aesthetics for nice trees are formalized and some algorithms for drawing nice trees are studied [109, 139, 142]. Planar graphs play an important role in graph theory, and there are many studies on planar drawings. Convex drawings of planar graphs were first studied by Tutte [134]. Chiba et al. present an algorithm for producing a convex drawing in linear time [32]. Becker and Hotz study the optimal layout of planar graphs with fixed boundary [10]. Another important class of graphs are acyclic digraphs which represent hierarchical structures. Information systems commonly use hierarchies for modeling. Carpano presents a method by which rank hierarchy in digraphs and number hierarchy in strongly connected digraphs and undirected graphs are automatically visualized [27]. Sugiyama et al. present a comprehensive approach to draw multilevel digraphs with reducing the number of edge crossings [124]. Some extended variations of Sugiyama's algorithm are proposed in [50, 92, 112]. Battista and Tamassia present efficient algorithms for constructing planar upward drawings of acyclic digraphs [9]. Hierarchical drawing of compound digraphs is studied in [123].

As for general undirected graphs, only a few algorithms are known because of the difficulties to optimize some drawing aesthetics such as symmetry, reduction of edge crossings, and uniform distribution of vertices. Eades presents a heuristic approach, called spring embedder, based on a physical model [39]. Our algorithm can be also viewed as one of the spring algorithms. A method for drawing general graphs symmetrically is proposed in [81]. A simple heuristic algorithm for placing the nodes one by one without backtracking is described in [141].

Tamassia et al. present a general strategy for orthogonal grid drawings based on a number of graph algorithms [129]. This orthogonal drawing algorithm is used to generate data flow diagrams [8] and entity-relationship diagrams [128]. In the field of VLSI design, some algorithms for laying out trees and planar graphs in area-efficient ways are developed [136].

CHAPTER 3

TRANSLATION INTO
PICTURES

In this chapter, we describe the proposed framework for visualizing abstract objects and relations. In our framework, the visual mapping mediates between relational structures and visual structures. We present the conceptual model of visual mapping, and realize this model by using Prolog and COOL.

3.1. An Introductory Example

We regard and discuss the visualization problem as the translation from textual languages into visual languages. As we have already stated, our purpose is to develop a general translation framework (see Fig. 1.1). In order to meet the requirement of generality, various kinds of translation must be taken into account. Indeed there are an infinite number of textual languages, from simple syntactic languages to natural languages. Each application system usually has its own textual language suitable for its processing. These languages are required to be translated into a variety of visual languages; e.g., many variations of trees and networks.

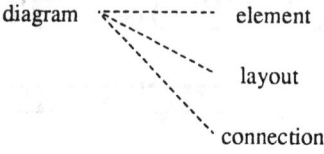

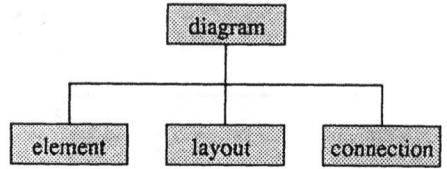

(a)   (b)

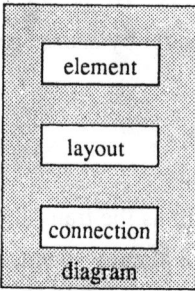

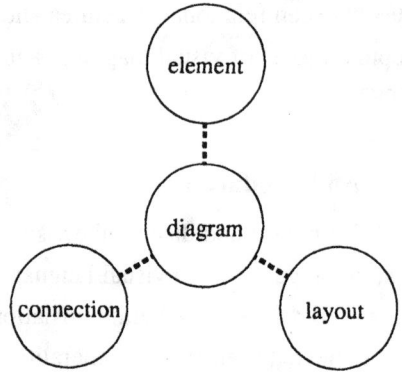

(c)   (d)

Figure 3.1:   Variations of drawing tree structures.

Desired pictorial forms would be different depending on the purpose of presentation even for the same data. Therefore the capability of changing pictorial forms easily is required of the system. We show one example. Suppose a simple tree structure in which the mother is *diagram* and the daughters are *element*, *layout*, and *connection*. Figure 3.1 shows four pictures (generated by TRIP) representing this structure. How is the structure translated into these pictures? Four abstract objects are translated into boxes bounding text strings in Fig. 3.1(a)-(c), and circles bounding text strings in Fig. 3.1(d). Note that boxes are invisible in Fig. 3.1(a). The translation of abstract relations is explained as follows. In Fig. 3.1(a), the mother-to-daughter relation is translated into horizontal arrangement of the mother and the first daughter, and the daughter-to-daughter relation is translated into vertical arrangement of three daughters. In Fig. 3.1(b), the mother-to-daughter relation is translated into the geometric relation by which the mother is placed above the daughters, and the daughter-to-daughter relation is translated into horizontal arrangement. In addition, the mother is connected to the daughters by dashed straight lines in the former picture, and by solid orthogonal lines in the latter picture. In Fig. 3.1(c), the mother-to-daughter relation is translated into the containment relation between boxes. In Fig. 3.1(d), three daughters are placed circularly around the mother with connecting lines. Users of TRIP have only to specify such translation rules for objects and relations in order to generate these pictures. All that users have to do to change a pictorial form is to change the visual mapping.

3.2. Translation Process

In order to realize the independence both of original textual representations and of target pictorial representations, we have introduced two intermediate representations between them. Figure 3.2 illustrates our visualization model. The translation process proceeds through the following four representations.

original textual representation

$\downarrow$

| Analyzer | $\longleftarrow$ - - - - - - - syntax data |

$\downarrow$

relational structure representation

$\downarrow$

| Visual Mapping | $\longleftarrow$ - - - - - - - mapping data |

$\downarrow$

visual structure representation

$\downarrow$

| COOL | $\longleftarrow$ - - - - - - - layout library |

$\downarrow$

target pictorial representation

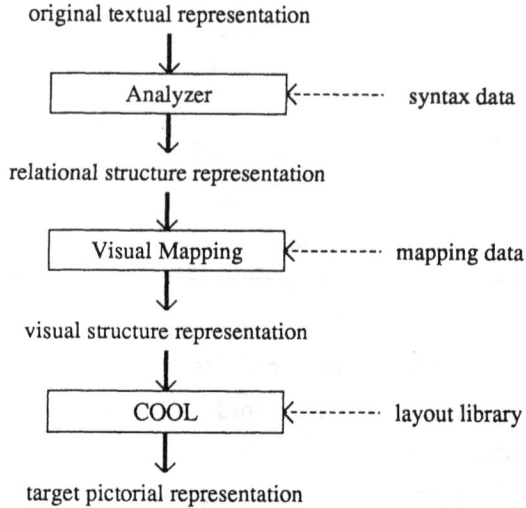

Figure 3.2: Proposed visualization model.

(1) original textual representation

Application programs or users deal with this representation of data. Any specific representation is not assumed. The input data for TRIP is a set of sentences of a textual language.

(2) relational structure representation

This level of representation expresses a relational (semantic) structure which is derived from the textual representation. A relational structure is represented by abstract objects and relations. Different textual representations are translated into this universal representation.

(3) visual structure representation

A visual structure means the relationships among the constituents in a picture, and is represented by graphical objects and relations. A relational structure is mapped to a visual structure by user-defined mapping data.

(4) target pictorial representation

This is the actual pictorial representation which users view. A pictorial representation is generated from the specification of a visual structure.

An analyzer parses a sentence and analyzes its semantics, and then outputs the relational structure representation. Note that a set of sentences is translated into a set of underlying semantic relations, which can be looked at as a (semantic) network. On the other hand, a grammar-directed approach by which a sentence is translated directly into a visual structure cannot handle network structures easily, as described later. The introduction of the relational structure representation enables us to handle general structures, not restricted within tree structures. Since analyzers are, of course, dependent on their textual languages, different parsers are necessary for respective languages. We can make use of parser generators such as YACC [61] in order to obtain the parser for a given language. Further if we get a special parser for a natural language, we can translate the natural language into pictures. In fact, we will show later the examples of pictorial interpretation of English sentences in Chapter 6. Since we leave the responsibility for preparing an appropriate analyzer to users for the present, we will not discuss more about this analyzing stage.

We have adopted Prolog to represent relational structures. In general, relational structures we treat here are network structures like semantic networks. Prolog has expressive power enough to describe network structures and process patterns on networks [75]. Pattern matching facility is convenient for specifying the visual mapping data. Abstract objects and relations are represented in terms of Prolog predicates. Graphical objects and relations are defined as special predicates which are the entries to COOL. The mapping from a relational structure to a visual structure is also described as a Prolog program. For the present, users actually specify the visual mapping in the programming environment of Prolog. We have a plan to develop a high-level user interface for specifying the visual mapping easily. A set of predicates for a visual structure can be viewed as a program for COOL. The kernel of COOL, which is outside of Prolog, solves constraints and generates a picture.

We can find an analogy between our visualization and machine translation of natural languages [120]. The usual translation process between natural languages consists of three successive phases: analysis (parsing), transfer, and synthesis (generation).[1] The source language is analyzed into the underlying semantic representation of a sentence. Then it is mapped to the semantic representation specific to the target language. Finally the corresponding target language sentence is generated from the representation. Our visualizing translation process consists of the phases just corresponding to analysis, transfer, and synthesis. This analogy justifies our claim that visualization is a sort of translation. In our model, the transfer phase, which we call the visual mapping, plays the role of mapping a relational structure to a visual structure. It is one of the most important characteristics in our model that the transfer phase is separated both from the analysis phase and from the synthesis phase and is designed to be controlled by users. COOL realizes the powerful synthesis phase in our model.

A Grammar-Directed Approach

We considered a method of translating an original textual representation directly into a visual structure [63]. In this method, a picture is generated according to the layout rules which are associated with the productions of a context-free grammar for the given data. Non-terminals correspond to graphical objects such as boxes and circles, and productions correspond to graphical relations among graphical objects. In order to realize such a visualization mechanism, we introduced an enhanced context-free grammar

---

[1] This approach is called the transfer approach. Another approach called the interlingua approach is known. In the approach, the source language is analyzed into a "deep representation" and then the target language is directly synthesized.

named "constraint grammar"[2] in which the relationships among the variables associated with non-terminals are expressed by constraints. Geometric relations are expressed as such constraints.

A constraint grammar can be regarded as a generalization of attribute grammar [2,71]. In an attribute grammar, the dependencies among attributes are described explicitly as semantic rules. Attributes are classified into synthesized attributes and inherited attributes according to their dependencies. It is therefore impossible to handle mutually dependent attributes, that is, cyclic dependencies in an attribute grammar. On the other hand, a constraint grammar can deal with mutually dependent variables (attributes) by expressing the relationships as constraints. In addition, a constraint grammar introduces a set of global variables. These constraints are solved by a constraint solver, which corresponds to an attribute evaluator in an attribute grammar. A constraint grammar is defined as a triple (G, V, C) such that;

(1) G is an underlying context-free grammar, $G = (N, T, P, S)$ where

N : a vocabulary of non-terminal symbols,

T : a vocabulary of terminal symbols,

P : a set of production rules,

S : a start symbol.

(2) $V(X)$ is a finite set of variables (attributes) associated with a non-terminal symbol $X \in N$. Let V_0 be a set of global variables.

(3) $C(p)$ is a set of constraints associated with a production $p \in P$. Let p be the form $X_0 \rightarrow X_1 \cdots X_n$, and then $C(p)$ is a set of constraints among the variables $V(X_0) \cup V(X_1) \cup \cdots \cup V(X_n) \cup V_0$.

Note that a constraint grammar can simulate an attribute grammar except for the difference of performance.

---

[2] Vander Zanden independently proposes a constraint grammar which can be used to model both the graphical display and dynamic behavior of an application [138].

Though this approach is an effective way of visualizing tree structures, it has a serious limitation that it can handle only tree structures essentially. In addition, it is difficult to relate the nodes far apart in a parsing tree. In order to visualize a network structure represented by some sentences, we need global structure information in specifying layout rules. Through this experience, we extended our idea and built up the above more powerful framework.

3.3. Conceptual Model of Visual Mapping

In order to clear the notion of proposed visual mapping, we describe the conceptual model on which the visual mapping bases. Up to this point, we have regarded informally a relational structure as abstract relations among abstract objects, and a visual structure as graphical relations among graphical objects. Before defining the visual mapping formally, we must model relational structures and visual structures. A visual structure represents what objects (components) are in a picture and how they are composed. It is very common to use the object-subobject or picture-subpicture hierarchy for structuring pictures in graphics systems [4, 48, 64, 130]. So hierarchy should be introduced explicitly into visual structures. We also introduce hierarchy into relational structures to represent n-level hierarchical structures straight-forwardly, though an n-level hierarchical structure can be replaced by a combination of two-level hierarchical structures. A relational structure and a visual structure are defined recursively as follows.

(Def. 3.1) A relational structure is defined as a pair (AO, AR) such that;
(1) AO is a set of abstract primitive objects (AP) and relational structures.
(2) AR is a set of relations (abstract relations) on AO^*.   □

(Def. 3.2) A visual structure is defined as a pair (GO, GR) such that;
(1) GO is a set of graphical primitive objects (GP) and visual structures.
(2) GR is a set of relations (graphical relations) on GO^*.   □

Sets of relations AR and GR include unary, binary, and n-ary relations on AO and GO respectively.

Now we can regard the visual mapping as the mapping from (AO, AR) to (GO, GR). First we consider the one-level visual mapping. In this case, it is assumed that there is no hierarchy either in relational structures or in visual structures, i.e., $AO = AP$ and $GO = GP$.

(**Def. 3.3**) A one-level visual mapping $v : (AP, AR) \rightarrow (GP, GR)$ is defined by the following mappings;

$$\alpha : AP \rightarrow GP,$$
$$\beta : AR \rightarrow GR.$$

Then,

$$v((AP, AR)) = (\alpha(AP), \beta(AR)). \quad \square$$

In the above definition, α and β are called object mapping and relation mapping respectively. An abstract relation $r \in AR$ among n abstract objects x_1, x_2, ..., $x_n \in AP$ is mapped to a graphical relation $\beta(r) \in GR$ among the corresponding n graphical objects, i.e.,

$$r(x_1, x_2, ..., x_n) \rightarrow \beta(r)(\alpha(x_1), \alpha(x_2), ..., \alpha(x_n)).$$

Next we extend the one-level visual mapping to the multi-level visual mapping. We can use the above relation mapping as it is. As for the object mapping, the recursive definitions of (Def. 3.1) and (Def. 3.2) must be taken into account. We introduce the general object mapping (α') to deal with this recursive structures.

(**Def. 3.4**) A multi-level visual mapping $v : (AO, AR) \rightarrow (GO, GR)$ is defined by the following mappings;

$$\alpha' : AO \rightarrow GO$$
$$\alpha'(x) = \begin{cases} \alpha(x) & \text{if } x \in AP \\ v(x) & \text{if } x \in AO - AP \end{cases}$$

where α is the same mapping as the one in (Def. 3.3),

$$\beta : AR \;\rightarrow\; GR.$$

Then,

$$v((AO, AR)) = (\alpha'(AO), \beta(AR)). \quad \square$$

According to the above definition, the visual mapping v is applied recursively to the hierarchical relational structure. Therefore the resultant visual structure becomes hierarchical.

A picture is often described hierarchically as a composition of subpictures. For example, EQN (a system for typesetting mathematics) [69] displays equations as a set of bounding boxes pieced together in various ways. In a VLSI layout system [90], a structured layout is described hierarchically as a composition of cells. By the multi-level visual mapping, the hierarchy in a relational structure can be visualized as the composite hierarchy in a picture.

3.4. Realization of Visual Mapping

We realize the conceptual model described in the previous section by using Prolog and COOL. An abstract object is represented by a term in Prolog. An abstract relation is represented by a compound term. The name of a relation corresponds to the functor of a compound term. Because an argument of a compound term can be also a compound term, a compound term satisfies the definition of (Def. 3.1). A visual structure is represented by the predicates for COOL. A graphical layout is specified hierarchically by the picture hierarchy mechanism in COOL. The specification of a subpicture, which satisfies the definition of (Def. 3.2), is started by the predicate *pstart*(*name*) and ended by the predicate *pend*. A subpicture can be referred to as the box object enclosing the component objects in it.

We show here actual mappings in order to give some guidelines for specifying the visual mapping. First a simple one-level visual mapping is taken up. We come back to the example in Fig. 3.1. Let the tree structure be described as the following Prolog predicates after the analyzing stage;

> *consist_of(diagram, [element, layout, connection]).*
> *is_object(diagram).*
> *is_object(element).*
> *is_object(layout).*
> *is_object(connection).*

The visual mapping for Fig. 3.1(a) is explained as follows. The object expressed by the pattern

> *is_object(X)*

is mapped to the box enclosing a text string expressed by

> *boxwithlabel(X, 60, 20, X, [invisible]).*

The last argument *invisible* means that the box is not drawn. The relation expressed by the pattern

> *consist_of(A, [H|L])*

is mapped to the following graphical relations;

> *horizontallisting([A, H], 60, [rigid]),*
> *verticallisting([H|L], 10, [rigid]),*
> *multi_connect([A], [H|L], right, left, [dashed, straight]).*

The first relation places the object corresponding to *diagram* on the left of the object corresponding to *element*. The next relation arranges the objects *element*, *layout*, and *connection* vertically from top to bottom. The last relation connects the right side of the object *diagram* to the left sides of the objects *element*, *layout*, and *connection* by dashed straight lines. We can obtain the picture in Fig. 3.1(b) by changing the above mapping. The object mapping is changed to

> *boxwithlabel(X, 60, 20, X, [visible]).*

The relation mapping is changed to

> *above([A], [H|L], 40, [rigid]),*
> *horizontallisting([H|L], 20, [rigid]),*
> *multi_connect([A], [H|L], bottom, top, [solid, orthogonal]).*

These graphical objects and relations are supported by COOL. COOL computes a layout of objects from graphical relations and generates a picture.

Next we take up a multi-level visual mapping for the tree structure. Suppose the case of visualing the following tree structure;

   tree(a, tree(b, tree(c, d, e), f), tree(g, tree(h, i, j), tree(k, l, m))).

Specifying the visual mapping recursively is a good way to handle such a recursive structure. Figure 3.3 shows a recursive visual mapping for this tree data. Each *tree* (X, Y, Z) pattern corresponds to a subpicture in which X is placed above Y and Z with orthogonal connecting lines. At this time, Y or Z is further mapped to a subpicture if it is the *tree* pattern. The visual mapping is thus applied to the given data recursively. Fig. 3.3 illustrates the resultant tree diagram. The detail of structuring mechanism in COOL will be described in Chapter 4.

As these examples show, users specify the visual mapping by relating the patterns on network structures to graphical objects and relations. The language facilities of Prolog such as pattern matching and backtracking make the specification of visual mapping concise.

```
%   A hierarchical visual mapping for the tree structure.
v( tree( X, Y, Z ) ) :-
    pstart( tree( X, Y, Z ) ),
    v( Y ),
    v( Z ),
    v( X ),
    horizontallisting( [Y, Z], 25, [top_align] ),
    above( [X], [Y, Z], 25, [ ] ),
    multi_connect( [X], [Y, Z], bottom, root, [thick, orthogonal] ),
    reference( tree( X, Y, Z ), root, X, top ),
    pend.

v( X ) :-
    boxwithlabel( X, 25, 25, X, [bound] ),
    reference( X, root, X, top ).
```

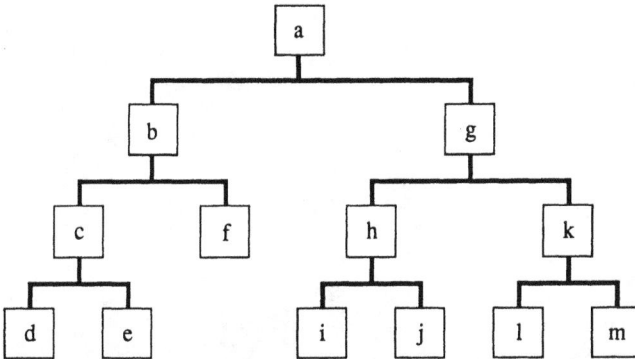

v(tree(a, tree(b, tree(c, d, e), f), tree(g, tree(h, i, j), tree(k, l, m)))).

Figure 3.3:   A tree visualized by a hierarchical visual mapping.

CHAPTER 4

A CONSTRAINT-BASED
OBJECT LAYOUT SYSTEM

The picture generation stage follows the visual mapping in our visualization process. In this stage, a visual structure is translated into a real picture. We have developed a constraint-based object layout system named COOL in order to handle the problem of determining a graphical layout from the visual structure representation. In this chapter, first we describe the COOL system, focusing on its characteristics. Then we explain how the picture generation is specified in COOL. The constraint satisfaction mechanism is also presented in detail.

4.1. The COOL System

In conventional graphics systems, users or application programs generate a picture by placing graphics primitives at certain positions and then translating, rotating, and scaling them [4, 45, 56]. However, it is troublesome and non-essential in many cases to specify the exact positions of graphics primitives, when users are more interested in the relationships among primitives than in the exact positions and orientations of individual primitives. The graphical layout problems treated here are the cases. In these cases, graphical relations among graphical objects should be handled elaborately. In COOL, the positions of graphical objects are computed automatically from the specified graphical relations by the system. Graphical relations are divided into geometric (positional) relations and drawing relations. Geometric relations are expressed as algebraic constraints among the variables which characterize the graphical objects. Line connections between objects and label drawings for objects and for connecting lines are supported as drawing relations.

In the course of specifying the visual mapping, users should concentrate on global layout scheme rather than local or componentwise constraints. In other words, the problem of over- and/or under-constrained systems should be handled not by users but by the visualization system. COOL does it. COOL is designed to be able to handle such an over-constrained system. In COOL, constraints are divided into two types, one of which must be satisfied exactly and the other needs to be satisfied not exactly but approximately. We call the former "rigid" constraints, and the latter "pliable" constraints. Pliable constraints are solved approximately by the least square method. Users can specify a complicated layout flexibly by associating important layout rules with rigid constraints and less important ones with pliable constraints.

Borning et al. propose constraint hierarchies for handling a problem of over- or under-constrained systems [20]. Constraint hierarchies include both required constraints and default constraints of differing strength. Stronger constraints are satisfied irrespective of the errors of weaker constraints. That is, a constraint hierarchy represents which constraints to be satisfied first in a dynamic environment. Our classification is, on the other hand, used to weight the errors of constraints. Though we have currently only two extreme classes (rigid constraints and pliable constraints), it is possible to divide pliable constraints into several classes of different weights. It could be implemented by multiplying the error of a constraint by its weighting factor in the least square summation.

In addition, COOL introduces the picture hierarchy. A set of graphical objects related by graphical relations may be bracketed as a subpicture which is a box enclosing them. Since a subpicture is treated as a graphical object, it can belong to another subpicture. The hierarchical structure represented by this picture hierarchy mechanism realizes the conceptual model of a visual structure described in Chapter 3. The system solves constraints hierarchically by traversing the picture hierarchy in a bottom-up manner.

COOL consists of three parts which are constraint solver, language interface, and graphics interface. The constraint solver is designed to be independent of the other two parts, and to be extensible. In the current version, constraints are restricted to be linear. TRIP uses the language interface for Prolog.[1] The drivers of graphics interface are prepared for different graphics devices. The pictures in this book were generated through the PostScript [1] interface.

4.2. Picture Generation Specification

In this section, we outline the picture generation specification in COOL. We are borrowing the programming environment from Prolog to specify the picture generation. The users' task for generating a picture is to generate graphical objects and to generate graphical relations among them by using special predicates for COOL. They have only to specify relative relations among objects without care of the order of relations, because the system computes a whole layout automatically from relative relations.

Before describing the functions of COOL, we present the fundamental principles of specifying layouts. We define several reference points for each graphical object, and connect objects by the relations among the reference

---

[1] We are using the SB-Prolog system which is a public-domain Prolog system originally developed at SUNY, Stony Brook [35].

points of them. Our layout specification is based on the following principles.

(1) Constrain the reference points of graphical objects to lie on a geometric curve (line, circle, ellipse, arc, spline, or etc) at equal intervals.

(2) Connect the reference points of graphical objects by a geometric curve (line, arc, spline, or etc) with or without an arrowhead.

For the present, we have implemented horizontal, vertical, diagonal, and circular arrangements as for the principle (1). In order to realize the arrangements along higher-order curves, we must introduce non-linear constraints into COOL. As for the principle (2), we have implemented line connections. Both straight line drawings and orthogonal line drawings are supported.

Graphical Objects

A graphical object is conceptually defined as the following three sets;
- a set of variables,
- a set of constraints,
- a set of drawing instructions.

Variables express the geometric attributes (such as position and size) of an object. Constraints express algebraic relationships among these variables. Drawing instructions express how to draw an object. Drawing instructions are sent to the graphics interface with the actual values of variables after constraints are solved. Graphical objects in COOL are similar to boxes in IDEAL [137]. They have local variables that are related to one another by simultaneous equations.

As examples, graphical objects BOX and CIRCLE are defined as Prolog predicates in Figure 4.1. A term is mapped to a box of given width and height by *box*, and is also mapped to a circle of a given radius by *circle*. BOX and CIRCLE have six internal variables respectively which are related to one another by intra-constraints. These variables express representative x- or y-coordinates of an object as illustrated in Fig. 4.1. As the modes for drawing instructions, four drawing styles are available: *invisible*, *bound*

```
% BOX( term, width, height, mode )
%     variables:  lx, rx, by, ty, cx, cy
%     available modes:  invisible/bound/fill/visible
%               default is visible(i.e. bound & fill)
box( Term, Width, Height, Mode ) :- map( Term, Object ),
     constraint( "$1.cx = ($1.lx + $1.rx)/2", [Object] ),
     constraint( "$1.cy = ($1.by + $1.ty)/2", [Object] ),
     constraint( "$1.lx + $2 = $1.rx", [Object, Width] ),
     constraint( "$1.by + $2 = $1.ty", [Object, Height] ),
     member( invisible, Mode ) -> map( Term, Object ),
          drawing( "box( $1.id, $1.lx, $1.rx, $1.by, $1.ty, invisible)", [Object] );
     member( fill, Mode ) -> map( Term, Object ),
          drawing( "box( $1.id, $1.lx, $1.rx, $1.by, $1.ty, fill)", [Object] );
     member( bound, Mode ) -> map( Term, Object ),
          drawing( "box( $1.id, $1.lx, $1.rx, $1.by, $1.ty, bound)", [Object] );
                    map( Term, Object ),
          drawing( "box( $1.id, $1.lx, $1.rx, $1.by, $1.ty, visible)", [Object] ).
```

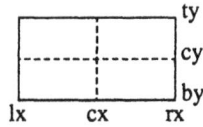

```
% CIRCLE( term, radius, mode )
%     variables:  lx, rx, by, ty, cx, cy
%     available modes:  invisible/bound/fill/visible
%               default is visible(i.e. bound & fill)
circle( Term, Radius, Mode ) :- map( Term, Object ),
     constraint( "$1.lx = $1.cx - $2", [Object, Radius] ),
     constraint( "$1.rx = $1.cx + $2", [Object, Radius] ),
     constraint( "$1.by = $1.cy - $2", [Object, Radius] ),
     constraint( "$1.ty = $1.cy + $2", [Object, Radius] ),
     member( invisible, Mode ) -> map( Term, Object ),
          drawing( "circle( $1.id, $1.cx, $1.cy, $2, invisible)", [Object, Radius] );
     member( fill, Mode ) -> map( Term, Object ),
          drawing( "circle( $1.id, $1.cx, $1.cy, $2, fill)", [Object, Radius] );
     member( bound, Mode ) -> map( Term, Object ),
          drawing( "circle( $1.id, $1.cx, $1.cy, $2, bound)", [Object, Radius] );
                    map( Term, Object ),
          drawing( "circle( $1.id, $1.cx, $1.cy, $2, visible)", [Object, Radius] ).
```

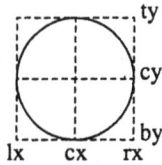

Figure 4.1: Definitions of graphical objects BOX and CIRCLE.

(boundary only), *fill* (interior only), and *visible* (boundary and interior). The default style is *visible*.

Special predicates *map*, *constraint*, and *drawing* which appear in the definitions of BOX and CIRCLE play the role of interface between Prolog and the COOL kernel. A term is mapped to a unique graphical object by *map*. Constraints and drawing instructions are generated by *constraint* and *drawing* respectively. For example, $box(a, 40, 20, [bound])$ generates the following constraints;

$$a.cx = (a.lx + a.rx) / 2$$
$$a.cy = (a.by + a.ty) / 2$$
$$a.lx + 40 = a.rx$$
$$a.by + 20 = a.ty$$

and generates the following drawing instruction;

$$box(a.id, a.lx, a.rx, a.by, a.ty, bound).$$

It is easy to add new objects to COOL by using these predicates, though only five objects BOX, DIAMOND, CIRCLE, ELLIPSE, and POINT are provided in the current implementation.

Geometric Relations

A geometric relation among graphical objects is expressed as extra-constraints among the variables of objects. COOL provides a variety of low-level geometric relations such as alignment relations and ordering relations of x- or y-coordinates. It also provides high-level relations by combining these relations.

A relation should be generic in the sense that it can be uniformly applied to all kinds of graphical objects.[2] In order to realize the generic property of relations, we pick up some geometric attributes which are

---

[2] There are, of course, object-specific relations such as adjoining relations in an arbitrary direction. Though these relations are required in some kinds of layouts, we have not added them to the system so far.

recognized to be common to all graphical objects. They are represented by the variables of the same name so that they can be referred to by graphical relations in an object-independent way. See a relation HORIZONTAL which constrains objects to lie on a horizontal line in Figure 4.2. It refers to the variable ty, by, or cy depending on the alignment mode. For example, $horizontal([a, b, c], [top\_align])$ generates the following constraints;

$$a.ty = b.ty$$
$$b.ty = c.ty.$$

Note that a HORIZONTAL relation can be used both for BOX and for CIRCLE, in fact for any object with the variables ty, by, and cy. Fig. 4.2 illustrates a HORIZONTAL relation between a box and a circle in three alignment modes.

Figure 4.3 shows the definition of a CIRCULARLISTING relation which constrains objects to lie on a circle around a specified object. A CIRCULARLISTING relation is expressed by $2n$ linear constraints among the variables cx and cy of objects, where n is the number of objects on a circle. For example, $circularlisting(o, [a, b, c], [])$ generates the six constraints;

$$a.cx = cos(360/3) * (b.cx - o.cx) - sin(360/3) * (b.cy - o.cy) + o.cx$$
$$a.cy = sin(360/3) * (b.cx - o.cx) + cos(360/3) * (b.cy - o.cy) + o.cy$$
$$b.cx = cos(360/3) * (c.cx - o.cx) - sin(360/3) * (c.cy - o.cy) + o.cx$$
$$b.cy = sin(360/3) * (c.cx - o.cx) + cos(360/3) * (c.cy - o.cy) + o.cy$$
$$c.cx = cos(360/3) * (a.cx - o.cx) - sin(360/3) * (a.cy - o.cy) + o.cx$$
$$c.cy = sin(360/3) * (a.cx - o.cx) + cos(360/3) * (a.cy - o.cy) + o.cy.$$

Note that the generated constraints are redundant because the relative circular relations of objects can be represented by $2n-2$ constraints. We intend to treat the objects on a circle equally by this definition when constraints are satisfied approximately. A CIRCULARLISTING relation can be also used for different objects as illustrated in Fig. 4.3. Other geometric relations are defined in the same way. Two modes *rigid* and *pliable* which represent the strength of constraints are commonly available for all geometric relations. We will show later how to use these modes.

```
% HORIZONTAL( [term, term, ... ], mode ).
%       available modes:  top_align/bottom_align/center_align(default)
%                         pliable/rigid(default)
horizontal( [_], _ ).
horizontal( [Left, Right | List], Mode ) :-
        hor2( Left, Right, Mode ), horizontal( [Right | List], Mode ).
hor2( Left, Right, Mode ) :-
        member( top_align, Mode ) -> hor2t( Left, Right, Mode );
        member( bottom_align, Mode ) -> hor2b( Left, Right, Mode );
        hor2c( Left, Right, Mode ).
hor2t( Left, Right, Mode) :- maplist( [Left, Right], Objects ),
        constraint( "$1.ty = $2.ty", Objects, Mode ).
hor2b( Left, Right, Mode) :- maplist( [Left, Right], Objects ),
        constraint( "$1.by = $2.by", Objects, Mode ).
hor2c( Left, Right, Mode) :- maplist( [Left, Right], Objects ),
        constraint( "$1.cy = $2.cy", Objects, Mode ).
```

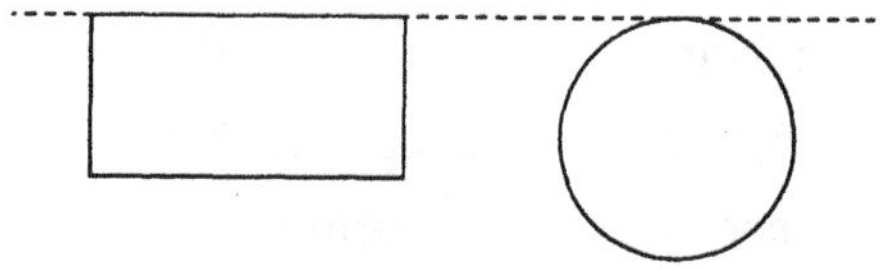

(a) top_align mode

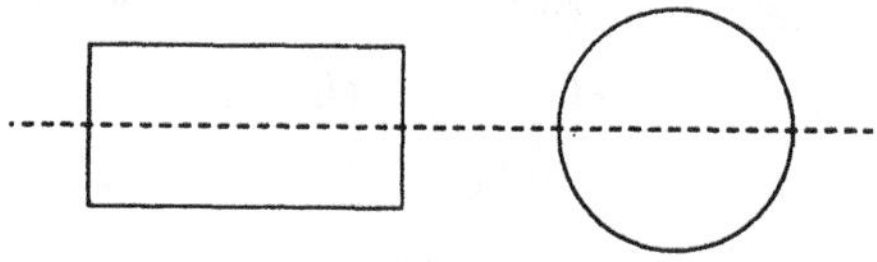

(b) center_align mode

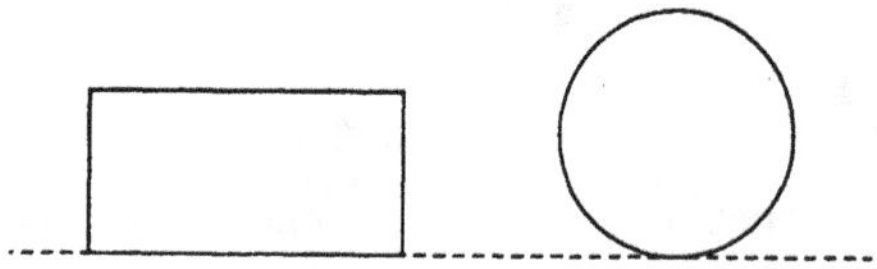

(c) bottom_align mode

Figure 4.2:   Definition of a HORIZONTAL relation.

% CIRCULARLISTING(origin, [term, term, ...], mode).
%   available modes: pliable/rigid(default)
circularlisting(Origin, List, Mode) :-
        count(List, Num), circularn(Origin, List, Num, Mode),
        item(1, List, First), item(Num, List, Last),
        cir2(Origin, Last, First, Num, Mode).
        % item(N, L, X) satisfies that the Nth item of L is X.

circularn(_, [_], _, _).
circularn(Origin, [First, Second | Rest], Num, Mode) :-
        cir2(Origin, First, Second, Num, Mode),
        circularn(Origin, [Second | Rest], Num, Mode).

cir2(Origin, First, Second, Num, Mode) :-
        maplist([Origin, First, Second], Objects),
        constraint("$3.cx = cos(360 / $1) * ($4.cx - $2.cx) - sin(360 / $1) * ($4.cy - $2.cy)
                + $2.cx", [Num | Objects], Mode),
        constraint("$3.cy = sin(360 / $1) * ($4.cx - $2.cx) + cos(360 / $1) * ($4.cy - $2.cy)
                + $2.cy", [Num | Objects], Mode).

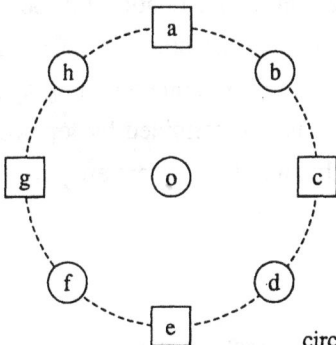

circularlisting(o, [a, b, c, d, e, f, g, h], [ ]).

Figure 4.3: Definition of a CIRCULARLISTING relation.

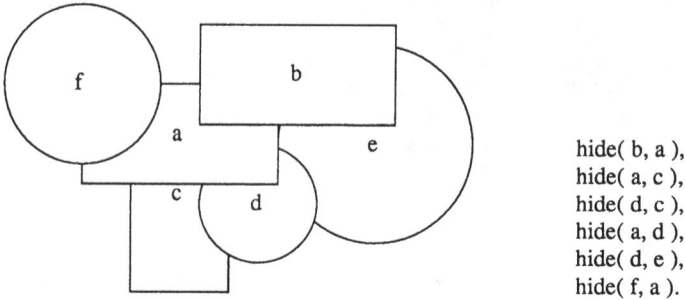

hide(b, a),
hide(a, c),
hide(d, c),
hide(a, d),
hide(d, e),
hide(f, a).

Figure 4.4:   An example of HIDE relations.

In order to deal with the overlapping problem that goes with drawing pictures in a two-dimensional plane, COOL provides a special geometric relation HIDE. A HIDE relation declares the depth relationship between two graphical objects. A hiding object obscures the other in the resultant picture. A set of HIDE relations defines a partial ordering among graphical objects. The depth order of graphical objects is determined by topological sorting [72]. Only partial orders embeddable into total orders are permitted. Figure 4.4 illustrates an example of HIDE relations.

Drawing Relations

A drawing relation among graphical objects generates a drawing instruction which refers to the variables of the objects. Drawing relations do not influence the procedure for determining the positions of objects, because they generate no constraints. The drawing relations currently available are label drawings and line connections. These relations are defined as generic ones.

A predicate *label* is prepared for drawing textual labels associated with graphical objects. A text string is placed inside the specified object depending on the mode (the third argument of *label*), which takes one of *top* , *bottom*, *left*, *right*, and *center*. The real position of a label is determined according to the variables of an object; e.g., *lx* and *cy* in *left* mode. Figure 4.5(a) illustrates the five cases of labeling a box. A textual label can be also drawn associated with a connecting line. A label is placed near the midpoint of a line, and on the upper side of it (on the left side in the case of a vertical line). As illustrated in Fig. 4.5(b), *connectwithlabel* draws a line with a label at its midpoint. In this example, it should be noted that POINT objects are labeled. It may seem tricky that the label specified in *left* mode is placed on the right hand of the point.[3]

Graphical objects can be connected by a line (*connect*) or an arrow (*arrow*). The connecting point of an object is specified as one of *top*, *bottom*, *left*, *right*, and *center*. The real position of a connecting point is determined by referring to the variables of an object like the position of a label. As drawing styles, *straight* and *orthogonal* modes are provided. In addition, two modes for line width (*thin* and *thick*) and three line types (*solid*, *dashed*, and *dotted*) are available. The default mode is *straight*, *thin*, and *solid*. In the orthogonal drawing, a polygonal line or arrow is drawn reasonably depending on the connecting points of objects. Fig. 4.5(c) and 4.5(d) show the orthogonal drawings. The drawing strategy is illustrated in Figure 4.6. One of the four possible routes is automatically selected according to the table in Fig. 4.6.

---

[3] The label is placed on the right of the point (lx, cy) in *left* mode irrespective of object types. In the case of a POINT object, (lx, cy) coincides with the POINT itself because the variables of a POINT object are constrained to satisfy equations $lx = rx = cx$ and $ty = by = cy$.

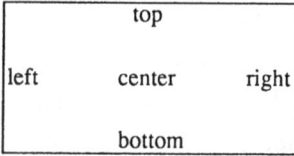

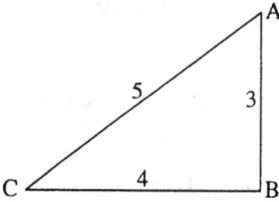

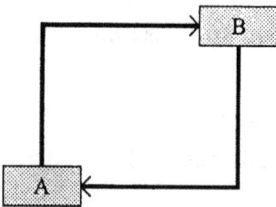

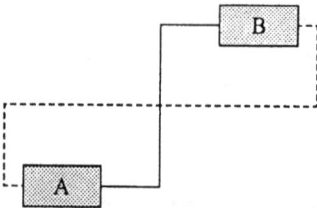

(a) box(object, 150, 75, [bound]),
     label(object, 'top', [top]),
     label(object, 'bottom', [bottom]),
     label(object, 'left', [left]),
     label(object, 'right', [right]),
     label(object, 'center', [center]).

(b) point(a), label(a, 'A', [left]),
     point(b), label(b, 'B', [left]),
     point(c), label(c, 'C', [right]),
     connectwithlabel(a, b, center, center,
                                    [straight], 3),
     connectwithlabel(b, c, center, center,
                                    [straight], 4),
     connectwithlabel(a, c, center, center,
                                    [straight], 5).

(c) box(a, 40, 20), label(a, 'A', [ ]),
     box(b, 40, 20), label(b, 'B', [ ]),
     arrow(a, b, top, left, [orthogonal, thick]),
     arrow(b, a, bottom, right, [orthogonal, thick]).

(d) box(a, 40, 20), label(a, 'A', [ ]),
     box(b, 40, 20), label(b, 'B', [ ]),
     connect(a, b, right, left, [orthogonal, solid]),
     connect(a, b, left, right, [orthogonal, dashed]).

Figure 4.5: Label drawings and line connections.

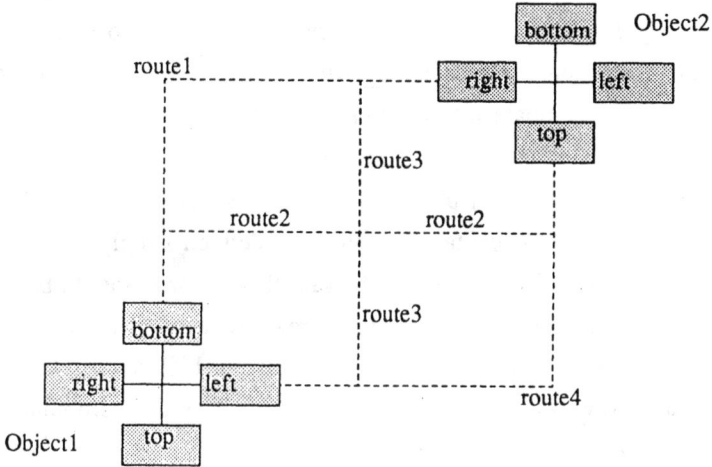

The route of an orthogonal drawing depends on the connecting points of objects. In the above case, the connecting route is determined by the variables X and Y where *connect(Object1, Object2, X, Y, [orthogonal])*, as follows.

X	Y	route
top, left or center	top, left or center	route1
top or left	bottom or right	route2
bottom or right	top or left	route3
bottom, right or center	bottom, right or center	route4

(When $X = Y = center$, route1 is selected.)

Figure 4.6: The orthogonal drawing strategy.

Basically a graphical layout is specified as a set of the above objects and relations. Figure 4.7 lists up the predicates for COOL in the current version. Relations *x_relation* and *y_relation* are provided as the most basic x- and y-coordinate relations. Relations *x_order* and *y_order* place objects at equal x- and y-coordinate intervals respectively. Relations *x_average* and *y_average* constrain the x- and y- coordinate center of an object to be x- and y-coordinate average of objects respectively. The relation *contain*, which constrains one object to contain the other, is defined simply by x- and y-coordinate relations. Though it may be said that *contain* should be treated as an object-specific relation, *contain* is realized as a generic relation at present. To make the specification concise, useful high-level relations are provided as shown in Fig. 4.7. They are defined as the combinations of these low-level relations.

The basic use of graphical objects and relations is illustrated in Figure 4.8. In these examples, low-level relations are used by intention. A larger example is shown in Figure 4.9. Many BOX objects are laied out under various graphical relations. In this example, 106 constraints among 106 variables are solved. In our visualization system, a program for COOL is generated by the visual mapping. However, COOL can be of course used separately to produce pictures as shown in Fig. 4.8 and 4.9.

1. Graphical Objects.

box(term, width, height, mode)	% BOX object
diamond(term, width, height, mode)	% DIAMOND object
circle(term, radius, mode)	% CIRCLE object
ellipse(term, xradius, yradius, mode)	% ELLIPSE object
point(term)	% POINT object

2. Geometric Relations.

x_relation(t1, t2, ref1, ref2, gap, mode)	% t1.(ref1) + gap = t2.(ref2)
y_relation(t1, t2, ref1, ref2, gap, mode)	% t1.(ref1) + gap = t2.(ref2)
x_order([t1, t2, ...], xgap, mode)	% t1.rx + xgap = t2.lx .....
y_order([t1, t2, ...], ygap, mode)	% t1.by - ygap = t2.ty .....
x_average(t1, [t2, ...], mode)	% t1.cx = (t2.cx + ...) / n
y_average(t1, [t2, ...], mode)	% t1.cy = (t2.cy + ...) / n
horizontal([t1, t2, ...], mode)	% t1.cy(ty,by) = t2.cy(ty,by) .....
vertical([t1, t2, ...], mode)	% t1.cx(lx,rx) = t2.cx(lx,rx) .....
contain(t1, t2, gap, mode)	% t1 contains t2
hide(t1, t2)	% t1 hides t2

3. Drawing Relations.

label(term, label, mode)	% label drawing
connect(t1, t2, from, to, mode)	% t1 is connected to t2 by a line
arrow(t1, t2, from, to, mode)	% t1 is connected to t2 by an arrow
connectwithlabel(t1, t2, from, to, mode, label)	% connect with a label
arrowwithlabel(t1, t2, from, to, mode, label)	% arrow with a label

4. High-level Relations.

boxwithlabel(term, width, height, label, mode)	% box & label
diamondwithlabel(term, width, height, label, mode)	% diamond & label
circlewithlabel(term, radius, label, mode)	% circle & label
ellipsewithlabel(term, xradius, yradius, label, mode)	% ellipse & label
pointwithlabel(term, label, mode)	% point & label
horizontallisting([t1, ...], gap, mode)	% horizontal & x_order
verticallisting([t1, ...], gap, mode)	% vertical & y_order
circularlisting(t1, [t2, ...], mode)	% t2, ... are on a circle around t1
diagonallisting([t1, ...], xgap, ygap, mode)	% x_relation & y_relation
above([t1, ...], [t2, ...], gap, mode)	% x_average & y_order
below([t1, ...], [t2, ...], gap, mode)	% x_average & y_order
leftof([t1, ...], [t2, ...], gap, mode)	% y_average & x_order
rightof([t1, ...], [t2, ...], gap, mode)	% y_average & x_order
between(t1, t2, t3, mode)	% x_average & y_average
multi_connect([t1, ...], [t2, ...], from, to, mode)	% connect t1, ... to t2, ...
multi_arrow([t1, ...], [t2, ...], from, to, mode)	% connect t1, ... to t2, ...
multi_hide([t1, ...], [t2, ...])	% t1, ... hide t2, ...

Figure 4.7: List of the predicates for COOL.

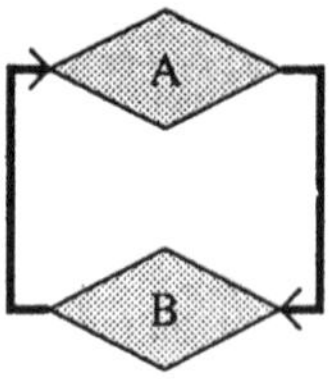

(a)   diamond(b, 60, 30, [visible]),
      label(b, 'B', [center]),
      diamond(a, 60, 30, [visible]),
      label(a, 'A', [center]),
      vertical([a, b], [ ]), y_order([a, b], 30, [ ]),
      arrow(a, b, right, right, [orthogonal, thick]),
      arrow(b, a, left, left, [orthogonal, thick]).

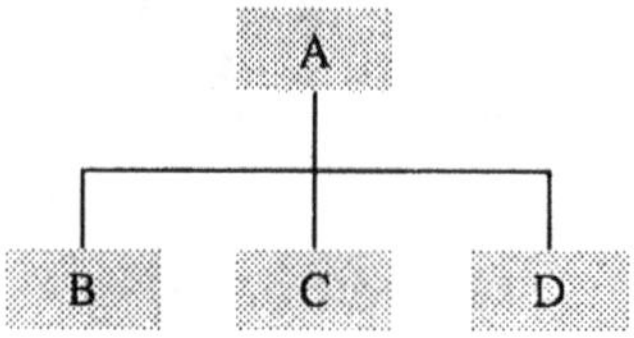

(b)   box(a, 40, 20, [fill]), label(a, 'A', [center]),
      box(b, 40, 20, [fill]), label(b, 'B', [center]),
      box(c, 40, 20, [fill]), label(c, 'C', [center]),
      box(d, 40, 20, [fill]), label(d, 'D', [center]),
      horizontal([b, c, d], [ ]), x_order([b, c, d], 20, [ ]),
      x_average(a, [b, c, d], [ ]), y_order([a, b], 40, [ ]),
      connect(a, b, bottom, top, [orthogonal, solid]),
      connect(a, c, bottom, top, [orthogonal, solid]),
      connect(a, d, bottom, top, [orthogonal, solid]).

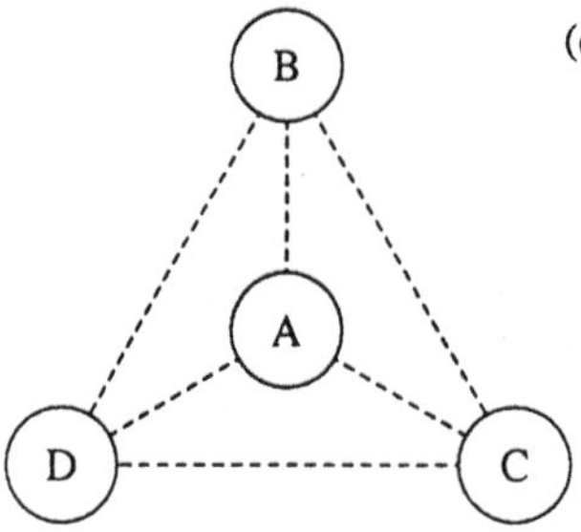

(c)   circle(a, 15, [bound]), label(a, 'A', [center]),
      circle(b, 15, [bound]), label(b, 'B', [center]),
      circle(c, 15, [bound]), label(c, 'C', [center]),
      circle(d, 15, [bound]), label(d, 'D', [center]),
      circularlisting(a, [b, c, d], [ ]),
      vertical([b, a], [ ]), y_order([b, a], 40, [ ]),
      connect(a, b, center, center, [straight, dashed]),
      connect(a, c, center, center, [straight, dashed]),
      connect(a, d, center, center, [straight, dashed]),
      connect(b, c, center, center, [straight, dashed]),
      connect(b, d, center, center, [straight, dashed]),
      connect(c, d, center, center, [straight, dashed]).

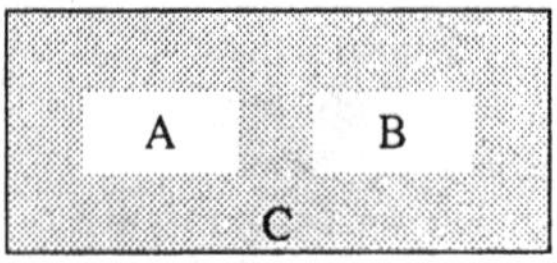

(d)   box(a, 40, 20, [invisible]), label(a, 'A', [bottom]),
      box(b, 40, 20, [invisible]), label(b, 'B', [bottom]),
      box(c, 140, 60, [visible]), label(c, 'C', [bottom]),
      contain(c, a, 20, [left_align]), hide(a, c),
      contain(c, b, 20, [right_align]), hide(b, c).

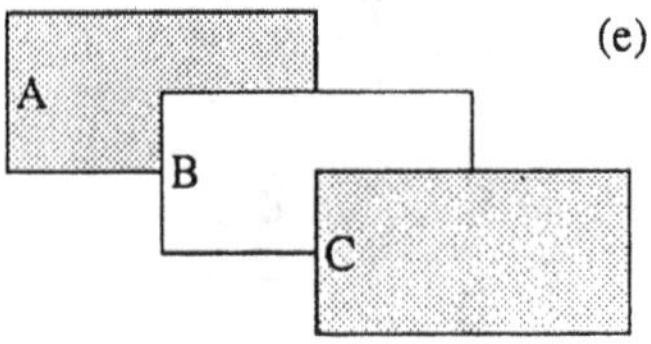

(e)   box(a, 80, 40, [visible]), label(a, 'A', [left]),
      box(b, 80, 40, [bound]), label(b, 'B', [left]),
      box(c, 80, 40, [visible]), label(c, 'C', [left]),
      diagonallisting([a, b, c], 40, 20, [ ]),
      hide(b, a), hide(c, b).

Figure 4.8:   Examples of picture generation in COOL.

%   diagram, text, structure, connection, layout, and element
boxwithlabel(o, 60, 20, 'diagram', [fill]), boxwithlabel(c1, 60, 20, 'text', [fill]),
boxwithlabel(c2, 60, 20, 'structure', [fill]), boxwithlabel(c3, 60, 20, 'connection', [fill]),
boxwithlabel(c4, 60, 20, 'layout', [fill]), boxwithlabel(c5, 60, 20, 'element', [fill]),
circularlisting(o, [c1, c2, c3, c4, c5], [ ]), verticallisting([c1, o], 60, [ ]),
multi_connect([o], [c1, c2, c3, c4, c5], center, center, [dashed]),
arrow(c1, c5, left, top, [orthogonal, dashed, thick]),
arrow(c3, c4, left, right, [solid, thick]),
%   tree, planar graph, and general graph
boxwithlabel(s1, 80, 20, 'tree', [bound, bottom]),
boxwithlabel(s2, 100, 40, 'planar graph', [bound, bottom]),
boxwithlabel(s3, 120, 60, 'general graph', [bound, bottom]),
contain(s3, s2, 0, [top_align, left_align]), hide(s2, s3),
contain(s2, s1, 0, [top_align, left_align]), hide(s1, s2),
horizontallisting([c2, s3], 30, [ ]), connect(c2, s3, right, left, [solid]),
%   straight line and orthogonal line
boxwithlabel(v1, 70, 20, 'straight line', [invisible]),
boxwithlabel(v2, 80, 20, 'orthogonal line', [invisible]),
horizontallisting([c3, v1], 30, [ ]), verticallisting([v1, v2], 10, [left_align]),
multi_connect([c3], [v1, v2], right, left, [orthogonal, solid]),
%   horizontal, vertical, and circular
boxwithlabel(h1, 60, 20, 'horizontal', [invisible]),
boxwithlabel(h2, 60, 20, 'vertical', [invisible]),
boxwithlabel(h3, 60, 20, 'circular', [invisible]),
horizontallisting([h1, h2, h3], 20, [ ]), above([c4], [h1, h2, h3], 40, [ ]),
multi_connect([c4], [h1, h2, h3], bottom, top, [orthogonal, solid]),
%   box, circle, and point
boxwithlabel(e1, 40, 20, 'box', [bound]),
boxwithlabel(e2, 40, 20, 'circle', [bound]),
boxwithlabel(e3, 40, 20, 'point', [bound]),
verticallisting([e1, e2, e3], 20, [ ]), rightof([c5], [e1, e2, e3], 30, [ ]),
multi_connect([c5], [e1, e2, e3], left, right, [dotted]).

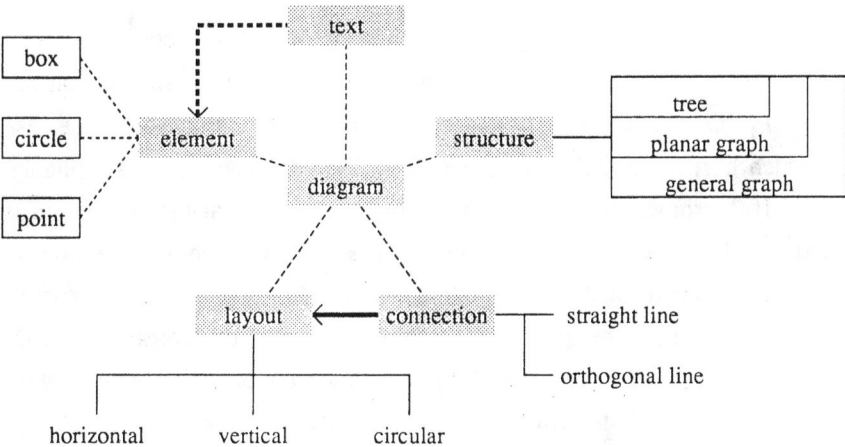

Figure 4.9: A diagram generated by COOL.

4.3. Advanced Features

COOL has some advanced features in addition to the basic layout facilities described above. In this section, we explain how to use pliable constraints and the subpicture structure. The integration of graph layout system into COOL is also described.

Pliable Constraints

We introduce pliable geometric relations expressed as pliable constraints into COOL in order to solve conflicting constraints. Pliable relations can be used mixed with rigid ones. Whether a geometric relation is rigid or pliable is specified as the mode *rigid* or *pliable*. (The default mode is *rigid*.) Conflicting pliable constraints are satisfied approximately by the least square method with rigid constraints satisfied exactly. Pliable relations are very useful for our purpose. The over-constrained cases sometimes occur in our layout problems, because it is difficult to map several abstract relations to non-conflicting two-dimensional geometric relations. In such cases, we can make the constraint systems solvable by converting some of the rigid relations corresponding to less important relations into pliable ones.

Figure 4.10 illustrates an example of pliable geometric relations. Eight CIRCLE objects are constrained by four geometric relations conflicting with one another. Obviously the constraints cannot be solved if all relations are rigid. In this case, the system reports the error. Fig. 4.10(a) shows the case in which horizontal listing relations are rigid and vertical ones are pliable. Fig. 4.10(b) shows the case in which only one horizontal listing relation is rigid and the rest are pliable. Contrarily Fig. 4.10(c) shows the case in which only one vertical listing relation is rigid. In these cases, the errors of pliable constraints are distributed over only the pliable constraints. Fig. 4.10(d) shows the case in which all relations are pliable. The resultant layout is balanced by distributing the errors of constraints over the whole.

Figure 4.11 shows another example. Eight CIRCLE objects and four BOX objects are laid out circularly. Fig. 4.11(a) shows the ordinary use of a

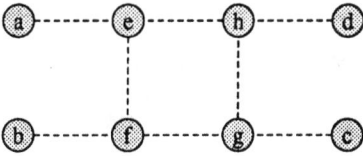

(a)   horizontallisting([a, e, h, d], 40, [**rigid**]),
      horizontallisting([b, f, g, c], 40, [**rigid**]),
      verticallisting([a, e, f, b], 40, [**pliable**]),
      verticallisting([d, h, g, c], 40, [**pliable**]).

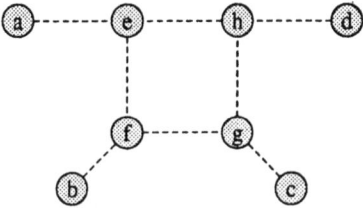

(b)   horizontallisting([a, e, h, d], 40, [**rigid**]),
      horizontallisting([b, f, g, c], 40, [**pliable**]),
      verticallisting([a, e, f, b], 40, [**pliable**]),
      verticallisting([d, h, g, c], 40, [**pliable**]).

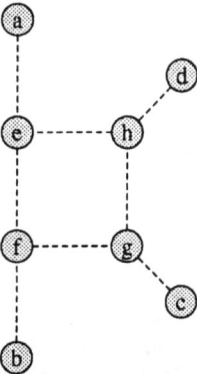

(c)   horizontallisting([a, e, h, d], 40, [**pliable**]),
      horizontallisting([b, f, g, c], 40, [**pliable**]),
      verticallisting([a, e, f, b], 40, [**rigid**]),
      verticallisting([d, h, g, c], 40, [**pliable**]).

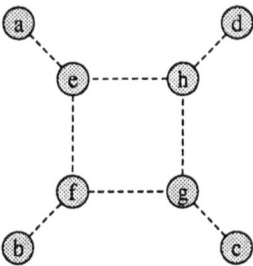

(d)   horizontallisting([a, e, h, d], 40, [**pliable**]),
      horizontallisting([b, f, g, c], 40, [**pliable**]),
      verticallisting([a, e, f, b], 40, [**pliable**]),
      verticallisting([d, h, g, c], 40, [**pliable**]).

Figure 4.10:   An example of pliable constraints (1).

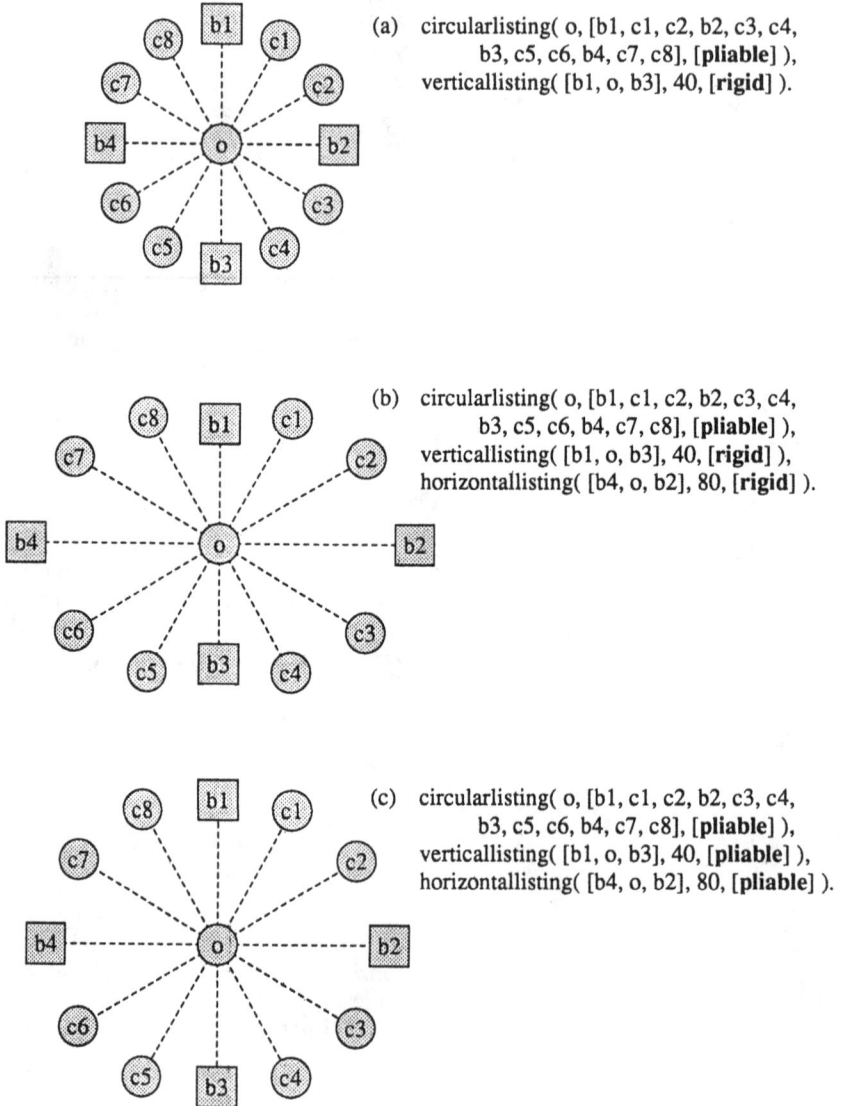

(a)   circularlisting(o, [b1, c1, c2, b2, c3, c4,
            b3, c5, c6, b4, c7, c8], [**pliable**]),
      verticallisting([b1, o, b3], 40, [**rigid**]).

(b)   circularlisting(o, [b1, c1, c2, b2, c3, c4,
            b3, c5, c6, b4, c7, c8], [**pliable**]),
      verticallisting([b1, o, b3], 40, [**rigid**]),
      horizontallisting([b4, o, b2], 80, [**rigid**]).

(c)   circularlisting(o, [b1, c1, c2, b2, c3, c4,
            b3, c5, c6, b4, c7, c8], [**pliable**]),
      verticallisting([b1, o, b3], 40, [**pliable**]),
      horizontallisting([b4, o, b2], 80, [**pliable**]).

Figure 4.11:   An example of pliable constraints (2).

circular listing relation. In this case, the constraints are satisfied exactly. Then, we add a horizontal listing relation which makes the constraint system contradictory. In Fig. 4.11(b), the circular listing relation is satisfied approximately. If we specify the all relations as pliable, the resultant layout becomes near the oval as Fig. 4.11(c) shows. As these pictures show, we can obtain pleasing approximate layouts by using pliable constraints in over-constrained cases.

Picture Hierarchy

It is a common way of building up a picture or a layout to divide it into some parts, construct each subpart, and combine them. For example, many graphics systems provide structure or segmentation facility by which graphics primitives are defined in a local coordinate space and then they are transformed collectively by coordinate transformations [4, 45]. A "block" in PIC [68] should be mentioned here. A set of graphical objects in a block can be placed by referring to their bounding box in PIC. We introduce such a bounding box hierarchy into our constraint-based object layouts. In COOL, a set of graphical objects and a set of graphical relations among them can be treated as a subpicture. A subpicture is regarded as a bounding box which encloses its component objects. As a subpicture itself is also a graphical object, subpictures may be nested.

Two special predicates *pstart* (*name*) and *pend* are provided for defining a subpicture. The objects and relations specified between *pstart* and *pend* are collected in a subpicture. A subpicture can be referred to in graphical relations by its name. We recall the example in Fig. 3.3. In this example, nested subpictures each of which corresponds to the pattern *tree* (X, Y, Z) are created by the recursive calls. Figure 4.12 illustrates the picture hierarchy in this example. The boxes bounded by dashed lines represent subpictures. In each subpicture, its subordinate subpictures are related geometrically by *horizontallisting* and *above* relations.

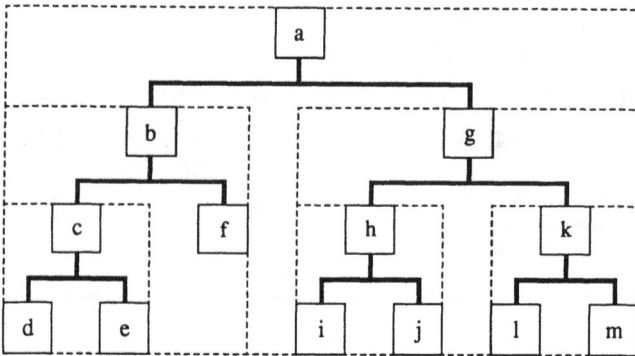

The boxes bounded by dashed lines represent subpictures.

Figure 4.12:   The picture hierarchy in Fig. 3.3.

COOL provides a function for declaring a reference point in a subpicture so that specific points can be referred to in graphical relations between subpictures. By a predicate *reference(newobj, newref, obj, ref)*, a reference point *newref* of an object *newobj* is defined as a reference point *ref* of an object *obj*. In the above example, *multi_connect* refers to the reference point *root* of a subpicture which is defined in the subpicture. Figure 4.13 illustrates an example of generating a bar chart. In this example, specific reference points of subpictures are aligned. The reference points named *alignment* of four subpictures are constrained to have the same x-coordinate. If required, a user-defined predicate *vertical_alignment* could be created in order to handle a series of *x_relations*.

We show another example of drawing trees by using subpictures. The problem of how to lay out a complete binary tree compactly by placing leaves throughout the chip has been studied in the area of VLSI layout. A simple way for this problem is the H-tree layout in which the nodes of a complete binary tree are placed recursively so that the tree looks like the letter 'H' [136]. It can be proved easily that the H-tree layout for a complete

```
%      subpicture for a bar
bar( X, Left ) :-
      pstart( X ),
      Right is 100 - Left,
      LeftWidth is 2 * Left,
      RightWidth is 2 * Right,
      boxwithlabel( [X I left], LeftWidth, 20, Left, [center, bound] ),
      boxwithlabel( [X I right], RightWidth, 20, Right, [center, bound] ),
      horizontallisting( [[X I left], [X I right]], 0, [ ] ),
      reference( X, alignment, [X I left], right ),
      pend.

pstart( bars ),
bar( a, 30 ),
bar( b, 65 ),
bar( c, 20 ),
bar( d, 55 ),
y_order( [a, b, c, d], 20, [ ] ),
x_relation( a, b, alignment, alignment, 0, [ ] ),
x_relation( b, c, alignment, alignment, 0, [ ] ),
x_relation( c, d, alignment, alignment, 0, [ ] ),
pend.
```

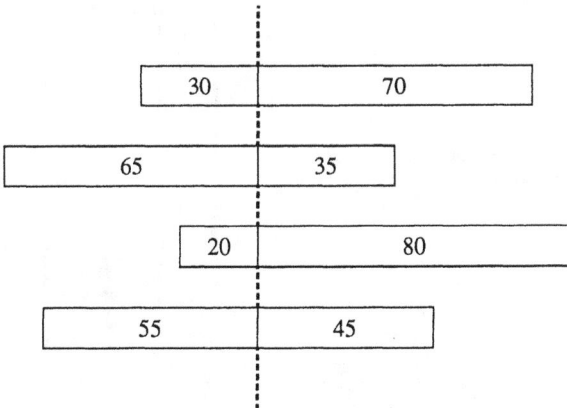

The right sides of left boxes of two bars are aligned by *x_relation*.

Figure 4.13: Geometric relations referring to specific reference points.

```
htree( X, 0 ) :-
      circlewithlabel( X, 7, 0, [invisible] ).

htree( X, L ) :-
      pstart( X ),
      SUBL is L - 1,
      NEWL is L - 2,
      htree( [a | X], NEWL ),
      htree( [b | X], NEWL ),
      htree( [c | X], NEWL ),
      htree( [d | X], NEWL ),
      circlewithlabel( [e | X], 7, SUBL, [invisible] ),
      circlewithlabel( [f | X], 7, SUBL, [invisible] ),
      circlewithlabel( [g | X], 7, L, [invisible] ),
      verticallisting( [[a | X], [e | X], [b | X]], 15, [ ] ),
      verticallisting( [[c | X], [f | X], [d | X]], 15, [ ] ),
      horizontal( [[e | X], [g | X], [f | X]], [ ] ),
      x_order( [[a | X], [g | X], [c | X]], 15, [ ] ),
      connect( [a | X], [b | X], center, center, [thick] ),
      connect( [c | X], [d | X], center, center, [thick] ),
      connect( [e | X], [f | X], center, center, [thick] ),
      pend.
```

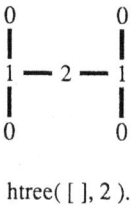

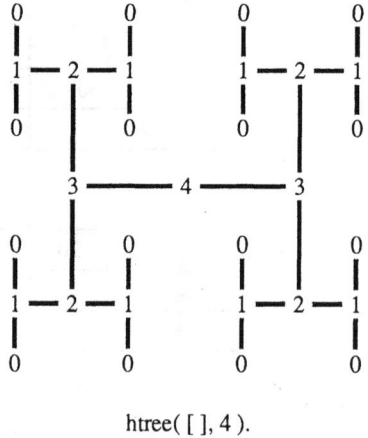

htree([ ], 2).

htree([ ], 4).

Figure 4.14:   H-trees.

binary tree of n leaves has $O(n)$ area. Figure 4.14 shows the specification
for generating a H-tree and the resultant pictures. In a subpicture which
corresponds to a 'H' pattern, four subordinate subpictures which correspond
to smaller 'H' patterns are arranged by some geometric relations. In COOL,
such a recursive layout can be specified easily by the picture hierarchy.

Integration of Graph Layout System

We integrate the graph layout system into COOL. The positions of
graphical objects can be determined by the use of our algorithm for drawing
general undirected graphs, whose details will be described in Chapter 5.
Geometric relations and drawing relations can be used together with this
graph layout. It may be, however, difficult to use geometric relations
besides graph layout constraints, because users can hardly forecast the resultant layout generated by the graph layout system.

A special predicate $adjacent(obj, obj, weight)$ which represents the
adjacency relation between two graphical objects is provided as the entry to
the graph layout system. The graph layout system collects these relationships among objects and computes the layout. Then the system outputs the
positional data in the form of linear constraints of cx and cy variables of
objects. COOL solves these constraints together with the constraints generated by geometric relations.

Figure 4.15 shows a network diagram whose layout is computed by the
graph layout system. Many CIRCLE objects are placed pleasingly by the
system. As this example shows, drawing relations such as label drawings
and line connections can be used with the graph layout.

Here we describe briefly how this graph layout facility serves the visual
mapping. We can visualize the relational structure by mapping abstract relations to rigid constraints in the simple cases, especially in the cases of tree
structures. However, it is difficult to specify the visual mapping by using
only rigid constraints in the cases of more complicated structures. In these
cases, we can usually visualize the structure pleasingly by mapping some of

the relations to pliable constraints. But there are still some cases in which one cannot notice a good visual mapping. It is in such cases that we use this graph layout facility by which a network structure is visualized as a network diagram.

%   Graphical Objects
Radius is 7,
circlewithlabel(a, Radius, 'A', [visible]),
circlewithlabel(g, Radius, 'G', [visible]),
circlewithlabel(h, Radius, 'H', [visible]),
circlewithlabel(i, Radius, 'I', [visible]),
circlewithlabel(m, Radius, 'M', [visible]),
circlewithlabel(n, Radius, 'N', [visible]),
circlewithlabel(b, Radius, 'B', [bound]),
circlewithlabel(c, Radius, 'C', [bound]),
circlewithlabel(d, Radius, 'D', [bound]),
circlewithlabel(e, Radius, 'E', [bound]),
circlewithlabel(f, Radius, 'F', [bound]),
circlewithlabel(j, Radius, 'J', [bound]),
circlewithlabel(k, Radius, 'K', [bound]),
circlewithlabel(l, Radius, 'L', [bound]),
%   Graphical Relations
adjacent(a, b, 1),   connect(a, b, center, center, [thick, dashed]),
adjacent(b, m, 1),   connect(b, m, center, center, [thick, dashed]),
adjacent(e, h, 1),   connect(e, h, center, center, [thick, dashed]),
adjacent(e, i, 1),   connect(e, i, center, center, [thick, dashed]),
adjacent(f, g, 1),   connect(f, g, center, center, [thick, dashed]),
adjacent(f, n, 1),   connect(f, n, center, center, [thick, dashed]),
adjacent(b, c, 1),   connect(b, c, center, center, [thick, solid]),
adjacent(c, d, 1),   connect(c, d, center, center, [thick, solid]),
adjacent(c, e, 1),   connect(c, e, center, center, [thick, solid]),
adjacent(c, f, 1),   connect(c, f, center, center, [thick, solid]),
adjacent(c, l, 1),   connect(c, l, center, center, [thick, solid]),
adjacent(d, f, 1),   connect(d, f, center, center, [thick, solid]),
adjacent(e, f, 1),   connect(e, f, center, center, [thick, solid]),
adjacent(j, k, 1),   connect(j, k, center, center, [thick, solid]),
adjacent(j, l, 1),   connect(j, l, center, center, [thick, solid]),
adjacent(k, l, 1),   connect(k, l, center, center, [thick, solid]).

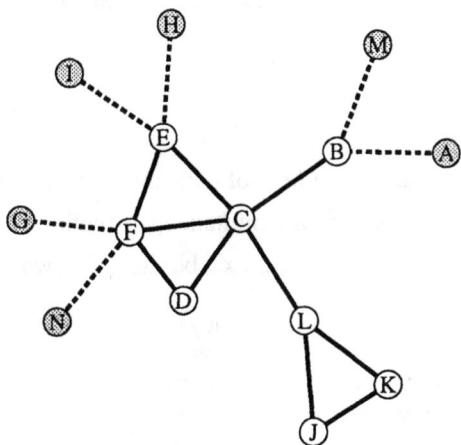

Figure 4.15: A network diagram.

4.4. Constraint Satisfaction

We present the constraint satisfaction technique adopted in COOL. It is difficult to handle constraint satisfaction (in a wide sense, problem solving) generally.[4] For example, even in the restricted case of only linear constraints, the constraint satisfaction problem would be as difficult as linear programming if inequalities are included. Symbolic manipulation systems such as MACSYMA [84] and REDUCE [57] can be used as general tools for solving constraints.[5] However, these systems work less efficiently owing to their generality. Accordingly constraint-based systems usually have domain-specific techniques. At present, several constraint solving techniques are known [80]; local propagation, relaxation, graph transformation, a simple equation solver, and a technique based on augmented term rewriting.

Our technique is based on a simple equation solver [36, 137]. The basic idea of our algorithm follows. Rigid constraints are eliminated like Gaussian elimination. After that, pliable constraints are solved by the least square method. This process is performed for each subpicture. First we describe the least square method for linear constraints, next we extend it to handle the equation systems including both rigid constraints and pliable constraints, and finally we present the hierarchical constraint solving mechanism for the picture hierarchy.

Least Square Method

The least square method has been used in the field of data analysis. We here use it for computing a least square solution of simultaneous equations. The problem to be solved is as follows. Let $x_1, x_2, ..., x_n$ be the unknown

---

[4] Gosling says that in its full generality, constructing a constraint satisfaction algorithm is a hopeless task [54].

[5] Recently there are some symbolic manipulation systems that can solve nonlinear polynomial equations by calculating Gröbner bases [24].

variables, and let $f_1, f_2, ..., f_m$ be the linear equations among them, i.e.,

$$f_j(x_1, ..., x_n) = a_{j1} x_1 + \cdots + a_{jn} x_n - b_j = 0 \quad (1 \le j \le m). \quad (4.1)$$

These equations are expressed in matrix form as $\mathbf{f} = \mathbf{A}\mathbf{x} - \mathbf{b}$, where

$$\mathbf{f} = \begin{bmatrix} f_1 \\ \cdot \\ f_m \end{bmatrix}, \quad \mathbf{A} = \begin{bmatrix} a_{11} & \cdot\cdot & a_{1n} \\ \cdot & \cdot\cdot & \cdot \\ a_{m1} & \cdot\cdot & a_{mn} \end{bmatrix}, \quad \mathbf{x} = \begin{bmatrix} x_1 \\ \cdot \\ x_n \end{bmatrix}, \quad \mathbf{b} = \begin{bmatrix} b_1 \\ \cdot \\ b_m \end{bmatrix}. \quad (4.2)$$

We define the square summation function as follows;

$$E = f_1{}^2 + f_2{}^2 + \cdots + f_m{}^2. \quad (4.3)$$

Our purpose is to compute the values of $x_1, x_2, ..., x_n$ that minimize E.

It is known that the least square solution of $\mathbf{A}\mathbf{x} = \mathbf{b}$ can be obtained by solving ${}^t\mathbf{A}\mathbf{A}\mathbf{x} = {}^t\mathbf{A}\mathbf{b}$ [107]. It is shown briefly as follows. A least square solution can be computed by solving the following n simultaneous equations;

$$\frac{\partial E}{\partial x_1} = \frac{\partial E}{\partial x_2} = \cdots = \frac{\partial E}{\partial x_n} = 0. \quad (4.4)$$

The partial derivative of E by x_i is computed from (4.3) as follows;

$$\frac{\partial E}{\partial x_i} = \sum_{j=1}^{m} 2 f_j \frac{\partial f_j}{\partial x_i}. \quad (4.5)$$

Then the equations (4.4) are expressed in matrix form as $\Delta E = \mathbf{J}\mathbf{f} = 0$, where

$$\Delta E = \begin{bmatrix} \dfrac{\partial E}{\partial x_1} \\ \cdot \\ \dfrac{\partial E}{\partial x_n} \end{bmatrix}, \quad \mathbf{J} = \begin{bmatrix} \dfrac{\partial f_1}{\partial x_1} & \cdot\cdot & \dfrac{\partial f_m}{\partial x_1} \\ \cdot & \cdot\cdot & \cdot \\ \dfrac{\partial f_1}{\partial x_n} & \cdot\cdot & \dfrac{\partial f_m}{\partial x_n} \end{bmatrix}, \quad \mathbf{f} = \begin{bmatrix} f_1 \\ \cdot \\ f_m \end{bmatrix}. \quad (4.6)$$

From (4.2) and (4.6), the equations (4.4) result in $\mathbf{J}\mathbf{A}\mathbf{x} = \mathbf{J}\mathbf{b}$, which is called normal equation. By the way, it should be noted that $\mathbf{J} = {}^t\mathbf{A}$ (${}^t\mathbf{A}$ is the transposed matrix of $\mathbf{A}$), because the partial derivative of f_j by x_i is a_{ji}, i.e.,

$$\frac{\partial f_j}{\partial x_i} = a_{ji} \quad (1 \le j \le m, 1 \le i \le n). \quad (4.7)$$

As a result, normal equation has the following form;

$$^tA\,A\,x = {}^tA\,b. \qquad (4.8)$$

The least square solution can be obtained by solving the equation (4.8) which can be solved by Gaussian elimination method. When $m = n$, the equation (4.8) gives the zero solution if A is non-singular (i.e., $rank(A) = n$). When $m > n$, the equation (4.8) gives the least square solution uniquely if $rank(A) = n$, otherwise it cannot be solved uniquely.

In the case of non-linear constraints, the problem is more intractable. Though the simultaneous equations of (4.4) may be solved by the Newton-Raphson iteration, there are some local minimums in general. It is difficult to compute the true minimum. This implies that the zero solution may not be computed even if it exists. Therefore it is a challenging extension to solve the least square solution of non-linear constraints.

Extension for Hybrid Solution

We have the constraints of two types which are rigid and pliable. We extend the above least square method for computing a hybrid solution which satisfies these constraints. Let $g_1, g_2, ..., g_p$ be the rigid constraints, and let $f_1, f_2, ..., f_q$ be the pliable constraints. The equations of rigid constraints are expressed as follows;

$$\begin{bmatrix} g_1 \\ \cdot \\ g_p \end{bmatrix} = B \begin{bmatrix} x_1 \\ \cdot \\ x_n \end{bmatrix} - c = 0. \qquad (4.9)$$

Now we assume that $rank(B) = r$ ($< n$). Then the variables $x_1, ..., x_r$ can be expressed as the linear combinations of $x_{r+1}, ..., x_n$ as follows;

$$\begin{bmatrix} x_1 \\ \cdot \\ x_r \end{bmatrix} = M \begin{bmatrix} x_{r+1} \\ \cdot \\ x_n \end{bmatrix} - d. \qquad (4.10)$$

By (4.10), $x_1, ..., x_r$ in the equations $f_1, ..., f_q$ can be eliminated. This process can be realized by Gaussian elimination. As a result, the equations of pliable constraints can be expressed as follows;

$$
\begin{bmatrix} f_1 \\ \cdot \\ f_q \end{bmatrix} = A \begin{bmatrix} x_{r+1} \\ \cdot \\ x_n \end{bmatrix} - b = 0. \tag{4.11}
$$

The least square solution of (4.11) can be computed by solving the corresponding normal equation (see (4.8)). After computing $x_{r+1}, ..., x_n$, we obtain the values of $x_1, ..., x_r$ by (4.10). By this extended version, the solution that satisfies the least squares of pliable constraints and that satisfies rigid constraints exactly is obtained.

Hierarchical Constraint Solving Mechanism

The constraint solving process proceeds by traversing the picture hierarchy in postorder. After the constraints in a subpicture are solved, the width and the height of the subpicture are computed. The size of a subpicture, that is, the size of the corresponding BOX object, is referred to when the constraints in its superordinate subpicture are solved. In this way, subpictures are processed from the leaves to the root. After this first traversal, the local solution of constraints in each subpicture is already computed. Next the final positions of objects in the picture are computed by translating subpictures in a top-down manner.

The constraint solver works for a subpicture as follows. Since a set of geometric relations describes only relative positions of graphical objects in a subpicture, two more constraints are usually required for determining x- and y-coordinates of objects. Therefore the following two constraints are automatically added to the equation system;

$$
(o_1.cx + o_2.cx + \cdots + o_n.cx) / n = center\_x
$$
$$
(o_1.cy + o_2.cy + \cdots + o_n.cy) / n = center\_y
$$

where $o_1, o_2, ..., o_n$ are all the objects in the subpicture, and $(center\_x, center\_y)$ is the coordinate of the center of display area. They mean to place the average point of all objects at the center of the subpicture. First each constraint is converted into the normal form, which is called, an ordered linear combination [36]. Two ordered linear combinations can be added together in linear time by merging them, because the variables in an ordered linear combination are ordered in a list. Keeping constraints in the form of ordered linear combinations, we implement the above extended least square method. Rigid constraints are eliminated in order based on Gaussian elimination.[6] If rigid constraints are contradictory, the system reports the error. (It is no problem that constraints are specified redundantly.) Then pliable constraints are solved approximately by the least square method. If the solution cannot be computed uniquely, the system reports the error.

The whole process of solving constraints in the picture hierarchy is summarized in a programming language form as follows.

(1) Bottom-up phase: solve(rootpicture).

solve(sp)
sp is a subpicture;
{
     let $sp_1, sp_2, ..., sp_m$ be the subordinate subpictures of sp;
     let $o_1, o_2, ..., o_n$ be the objects in sp;
     solve(sp_1);
     solve(sp_2);

     ....
     solve(sp_m);
     add two constraints:
        $(o_1.cx + o_2.cx + \cdots + o_n.cx) / n = center\_x$,
        $(o_1.cy + o_2.cy + \cdots + o_n.cy) / n = center\_y$;
     convert all constraints into the form of ordered linear combinations;
     eliminate rigid constraints;
     solve pliable constraints;
     compute the width of sp:

---

[6] We can extend this process so that it can solve slightly non-linear simultaneous equations by using the technique presented in [137].

$$\max_i o_i.rx \ - \ \min_i o_i.lx \ ;$$

compute the height of sp :

$$\max_i o_i.ty \ - \ \min_i o_i.by \ ;$$

}

(2) Top-down phase: translate(rootpicture).

translate(sp)
sp is a subpicture;
{

    let $sp_1, sp_2, ..., sp_m$ be the subordinate subpictures of sp ;
    let $o_1, o_2, ..., o_n$ be the objects in sp ;
    translate $o_1, o_2, ..., o_n$;
    translate(sp_1);
    translate(sp_2);

    ....

    translate(sp_m);

}

Note that the system executes *max* and *min* operations to compute the size of a subpicture while solving constraints subpicture by subpicture. If we try to solve all constraints in all subpictures at a time, we must solve these *max* and *min* constraints with other constraints at the same time. It is almost impossible to solve *max* and *min* constraints efficiently. In this sense, our hierarchical solving mechanism can be said to be an effective method for introducing *max* and *min* operations into constraint systems.

4.5. Summary

We have presented a constraint-based object layout system named COOL. Users of COOL specify the picture generation by using graphical objects and graphical relations. We have introduced pliable constraints to visualize complicated multi-dimensional relations in a two-dimensional restricted space. We have also introduced the picture hierarchy mechanism by which graphical objects connected by graphical relations are handled collectively. In addition, we have combined COOL with the graph layout system based on our graph drawing algorithm.

The current version of COOL has many things to be extended. First more reference points should be added to a graphical object. In addition to reference points, we are going to introduce the geometric attributes such as shape, size, and direction of an object. These attributes should be also controlled by geometric relations. Secondly we should provide high-level drawing relations which draw labels and lines depending on the positions of objects. For example, when a relation draws a line between two objects, it would be better that the relation could automatically select the nearest reference points of them and select an appropriate route. Further, it is a challenging extension to draw labels and lines so that they could not overlap other graphical objects. The optimization of labeling and routing involves several layout problems in computational geometry [104].

We have defined graphical relations as generic relations in order to apply them to all kinds of graphical objects. We are noting that CLOS [16, 67] is suitable for implementing COOL. Graphical objects can be defined on the class hierarchy, and the generic graphical relations can be easily realized as the generic functions in CLOS.

CHAPTER 5

AN ALGORITHM FOR DRAWING
GENERAL UNDIRECTED GRAPHS

In this chapter, we describe an algorithm for drawing general undirected graphs. The graph layout system which implemented this algorithm is integrated into COOL. In TRIP, we can visualize a network structure as a network diagram by using a special visual mapping which is the entry to the graph layout system.

The pictures that viewers want, of course, depend on the purpose and the structure. Here we consider the case in which viewers have no a priori information about the structure and want a general picture in order to understand the overall image of it. Main difficulty of this problem is how to formulate the criteria of nice drawings in a simple form. First we describe the conditions of general pictures of graphs, and also present our method for satisfying these conditions. Next we describe the details of our algorithm for computing a layout of vertices, and then we show some examples. Finally we apply the method to radial drawings and layered drawings.

5.1. Graph Drawing Problem and Spring Model

Graphs (networks) are very common data structures handled in computers. Diagrams are widely used to represent the graph structures visually in many information systems. Basic graph drawing algorithms are necessary for automatically drawing the diagrams which are, for example, state diagrams, data flow diagrams, Petri nets, and entity-relationship diagrams.

As we have surveyed the related work in this area in Chapter 2, there have been only a few algorithms for drawing general undirected graphs. We present a simple but successful algorithm for drawing undirected graphs and weighted graphs. The basic idea of our algorithm follows. We regard the desirable "geometric" (Euclidean) distance between two vertices in the drawing as the "graph theoretic" distance between them in the corresponding graph. We introduce a virtual dynamic system in which every two vertices are connected by a "spring" of such desirable length. Then, we regard the optimal layout of vertices as the state in which the total spring energy of the system is minimal.

The "spring" idea for drawing general graphs was introduced in [39], and similar methods were used for drawing planar graphs with fixed boundary [10, 134]. In VLSI circuit design, a similar force-directed approach to automated placement of modules has been studied [21, 105]. Our work brings a new significant result in the graph drawing based on a spring model.

Conditions of Nice drawings

We will clarify the graph drawing problem we treat here. There are a lot of ways to visualize graph structures. In some methods, the positions of vertices are restricted: e.g., they are placed on grid points, concentric circles, or parallel lines. Edges are drawn as straight lines, polygonal lines, or curves. In addition, there are various graphical rhetoric techniques using colors, line styles, symbols and etc. We treat here the drawings in which the positions of vertices are not restricted and edges are drawn as straight lines. Then, what we should do is to determine the positions of vertices for a given graph G. (G is expressed by the set of vertices V and the set of edges E). At the end of this chapter, we will handle the drawings in which vertices are constrained to lie on concentric circles or on parallel lines. We assume that a given graph is connected. The picture of a disconnected graph is obtained by drawing its connected components separately. A graph can be decomposed into connected components in running time $O(|V|+|E|)$ [114].

First of all we must discuss the fundamental conditions of general views of a graph. The graph structure encompasses so many kinds of structures, from trees to complete graphs, that it is difficult to find out the common criteria of nice drawings. However, the following two requirements in drawing graphs are commonly admitted [27, 140]. One is to reduce the number of edge crossings, and the other is to distribute vertices and edges uniformly. However it is difficult to reduce the number of edge crossings. In fact, the problem of minimizing the number of edge crossings for general graphs is NP-complete [52]. In addition, it can be shown that the reduction of edge crossings is not necessarily a good criterion as follows. Pictures with minimal number of edge crossings are not always the best. For example, Figure 5.1 shows three pictures of the complete 5-vertex graph K_5. Almost all people think Fig. 5.1(a) is the best for the representation of the internal structure, though it has five edge crossings. Fig. 5.1(b) and 5.1(c) sacrifice symmetry for the reduction of edge crossings. Figure 5.2 shows another example in which a 16-vertex graph is drawn differently. If they are not interested in planarity, people think Fig. 5.2(a) is better than Fig. 5.2(b). Symmetric structures should be drawn as symmetric pictures because symmetry is a valuable characteristic of structures. These examples suggest that the total balance of layout is as important as or even more important than the reduction of edge crossings for human understanding. The latter condition (uniformity) does imply the total balance. Accordingly our attention is now paid to how to judge that a layout is balanced totally. In our model, the total balance condition is formulated as the square summation of the differences between desirable distances and real ones for all pairs of vertices.

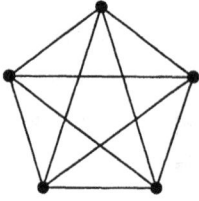

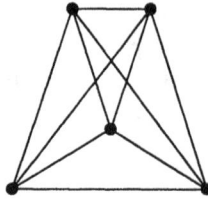

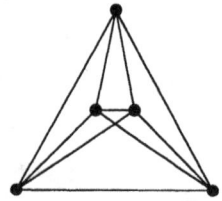

(a) 5 edge crossings   (b) 3 edge crossings   (c) 1 edge crossing

Figure 5.1:   Three pictures of the complete 5-vertex graph.

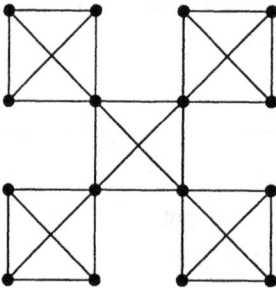

(a) 5 edge crossings   (b) no edge crossings

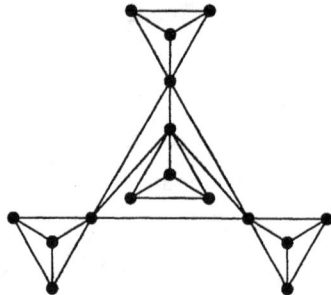

Figure 5.2:   Symmetric and planar drawings of a 16-vertex graph.

Spring Model

We introduce a dynamic system in which n $(=|V|)$ particles are mutually connected by springs. Let $p_1, p_2, ..., p_n$ be the particles in a plane corresponding to the vertices $v_1, v_2, ..., v_n \in V$ respectively. We relate the balanced layout of vertices to the dynamically balanced spring system. As a result, the degree of imbalance can be formulated as the total energy of springs, i.e.,

$$E = \sum_{i=1}^{n-1} \sum_{j=i+1}^{n} \frac{1}{2} k_{ij} (|p_i - p_j| - l_{ij})^2. \qquad (5.1)$$

Pleasing layouts can be obtained by decreasing E, and then the best layout corresponds to the state with minimum E in our model. The original length l_{ij} of the spring between p_i and p_j, which corresponds to the desirable length between them in the drawing, is determined as follows. The distance d_{ij} between two vertices v_i and v_j in a graph is defined as the length of the shortest path(s) between v_i and v_j [11]. Then, we define l_{ij} as

$$l_{ij} = L \times d_{ij} \qquad (5.2)$$

where L is the desirable length of a single edge in the display plane. When the display space is restricted, it is convenient to determine L depending on the diameter (i.e., the distance between the farthest pairs [11]) of a given graph. That is,

$$L = L_0 / \max_{i<j} d_{ij} \qquad (5.3)$$

where L_0 is the length of a side of display square area. The parameter k_{ij}, which is the strength of the spring between p_i and p_j, is determined as follows. The expression (5.1) can be regarded as the square summation of the differences between desirable distances and real ones for all pairs of particles. From this point of view, the difference per unit length is better to be used in (5.1). Then, we define k_{ij} as

$$k_{ij} = K / d_{ij}^2 \qquad (5.4)$$

where K is a constant (e.g., $K = 1$). The parameters l_{ij} and k_{ij} are symmetric, i.e., $l_{ij} = l_{ji}$ and $k_{ij} = k_{ji}$ $(i \neq j)$.

In this spring system, each pair of particles p_i and p_j are forced to keep Euclidean distance l_{ij} by the tension of a spring. As a result, the density of particles does not become large. We can obtain pleasing layouts by decreasing E. We will present a method of computing a local minimum of E from a certain initial state in the next section. In this method, the process by which a particle is moved to a stable position is iterated until all particles become dynamically stable. It should be also noted that needless edge crossings can be avoided to some extent by minimizing E. It is explained as follows. Figure 5.3(a) shows a part of a graph in which edges AC and BD intersect. The spring between A and D $(B$ and $C)$ is longer than the spring between A and C $(B$ and $D)$. Then, taking notice of only these four vertices, the energy E of Fig. 5.3(b) in which C and D are exchanged is smaller than that of Fig. 5.3(a) in many cases.

Symmetric Drawing Property

As we have described above, symmetry is the best general criterion of nice drawings in our view. Some algorithms really try to draw graphs symmetrically. Lipton et al. propose a method of drawing a graph with as many symmetries as possible [81]. Manning and Atallah present efficient algorithms for producing symmetric drawings of trees [87] and of outerplanar graphs [88]. Here we analyze the symmetric drawing property of our algorithm. Since pictures are drawn in a two-dimensional plane, only geometric (Euclidean) symmetries, i.e., reflections and rotations, can be expressed. We prove that there exists a symmetric "stable" layout in our spring model for a graph with some automorphisms. A layout is "stable" if and only if the total energy E of the layout is locally minimized; in other words, all springs are balanced. However, since there exists generally more than one stable layout, the resultant layout generated by our algorithm depends on the initial layout.

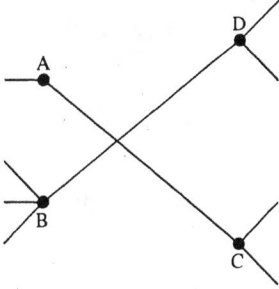

(a) AC and BD intersect   (b) AC and BD don't intersect

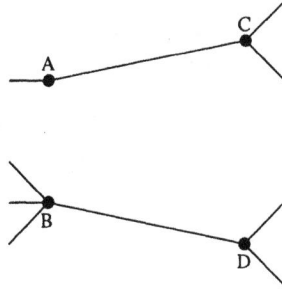

Figure 5.3: Two pictures of a subgraph which has two edges AC and BD.

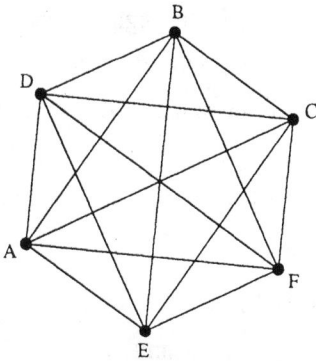

(a) hexagon type   (b) pentagon type

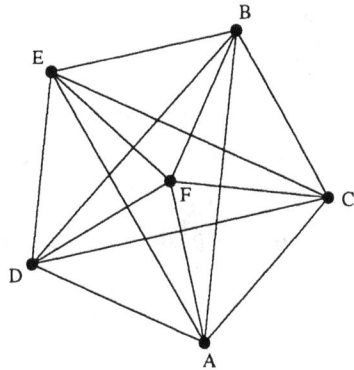

Figure 5.4: Two stable layouts of the complete 6-vertex graph.

In the following, we discuss that a graph which has a reflection with at most one fixed point has a stable layout with a line of reflection, and that a graph which has a rotation with at most one fixed point has a circular stable layout.

(1) **A graph which has a fixed-point-free reflection has a stable layout with a line of reflection.**

A fixed-point-free reflection is expressed as the product of independent transpositions as follows;

$$\sigma = (s_1, t_1)(s_2, t_2) \cdots (s_m, t_m)$$

where $S = \{s_1, s_2, \cdots, s_m\}$, $T = \{t_1, t_2, \cdots, t_m\}$, and $V = S \cup T$ $(n = 2m)$. Consider a layout in which each vertex $s_i \in S$ is mapped into $t_i \in T$ by a line reflection. The resultant forces of s_i and t_i are symmetric about the line in this layout. Therefore, from the standpoint of pure dynamics, we can say that there exists a stable state symmetric about the line. Obviously the line of reflection goes through the center of the layout, which is defined as the average position of all vertices.

(2) **A graph which has a reflection with a fixed point has a stable layout with a line of reflection.**

A reflection with a fixed point is expressed as the product of independent transpositions as follows;

$$\sigma = (s_1, t_1)(s_2, t_2) \cdots (s_m, t_m)(f)$$

where $S = \{s_1, s_2, \cdots, s_m\}$, $T = \{t_1, t_2, \cdots, t_m\}$, and $V = S \cup T \cup \{f\}$ $(n = 2m+1)$. Consider a layout in which each vertex $s_i \in S$ is mapped into $t_i \in T$ by the line reflection like the previous case. Since fixed point f is mapped into itself, f should lie on the line. The dynamic system of this layout is also symmetric about the line. Therefore it is sure that there exists a stable state symmetric about the line.

(3) **A graph which has a fixed-point-free rotation has a circular stable layout.**

A fixed-point-free rotation is expressed as follows;

$$\sigma = (s_1, s_2, \cdots, s_n)$$

where $V = \{s_1, s_2, \cdots, s_n\}$. Consider a layout in which vertices s_1, s_2, ..., s_n are placed on a circle at equal intervals in this order. In the dynamic system of this layout, the resultant forces of vertices are of equal strength, and direct to or from the center of the circle. Therefore we can obtain a stable layout by choosing a circle of an appropriate radius.

(4) **A graph which has a rotation with a fixed point has a circular stable layout.**

A rotation with a fixed point is expressed as follows;

$$\sigma = (s_1, s_2, \cdots, s_{n-1})(f)$$

where $V = \{s_1, s_2, \cdots, s_{n-1}\} \cup \{f\}$. Consider a layout in which vertices $s_1, s_2, ..., s_{n-1}$ are placed on a circle at equal intervals in this order and fixed point f is placed at the center of the circle. The dynamic system of this layout is similar to the one in the previous case. Therefore we can obtain a stable layout by choosing a circle of an appropriate radius.

It is not necessary true that there exists a stable layout with a line of reflection for a graph which has a reflection with some fixed points. It depends on the adjacent relations among the vertices corresponding to fixed points. Figure 5.4 shows two stable layouts of the complete 6-vertex graph. In fact, the layout process converges to one of these layouts depending on the initial layout. (The energy E in Fig. 5.4(a) is a little smaller than that in Fig. 5.4(b).) This fact is explained immediately by the above discussion about rotations.

5.2. Graph Drawing Algorithm

Local Minimization of Global Energy

We prepare some definitions for describing the algorithm and outline our method. The position of a particle in a plane is expressed by x- and y-coordinate values. Let (x_1, y_1), (x_2, y_2), ..., (x_n, y_n) be the coordinate variables of particles $p_1, p_2, ..., p_n$ respectively. Then, we rewrite the energy E defined as (5.1) by using these $2n$ variables as follows;

$$E = \sum_{i=1}^{n-1} \sum_{j=i+1}^{n} \frac{1}{2} k_{ij} \{(x_i - x_j)^2 + (y_i - y_j)^2 + l_{ij}^2 - 2l_{ij}\sqrt{(x_i - x_j)^2 + (y_i - y_j)^2}\}. \quad (5.5)$$

Our purpose is to compute the values of these variables that minimize $E(x_1, x_2, ..., x_n, y_1, y_2, ..., y_n)$. (Hereafter the parameters of the function E are omitted.) It is, however, quite difficult to compute the minimum, so we instead compute a local minimum. Later we will improve this local minimization so that E can converge to the smaller local minimum.

We present a method of computing a local minimum of E from a certain initial state based on the Newton-Raphson method [132]. The necessary condition of a local minimum is as follows;

$$\frac{\partial E}{\partial x_m} = \frac{\partial E}{\partial y_m} = 0 \quad \text{for } 1 \leq m \leq n. \quad (5.6)$$

The state satisfying (5.6) corresponds to the dynamic state in which the forces of all springs are balanced. The partial derivatives of (5.5) by x_m and y_m are as follows;

$$\frac{\partial E}{\partial x_m} = \sum_{i \neq m} k_{mi} \{(x_m - x_i) - \frac{l_{mi}(x_m - x_i)}{\{(x_m - x_i)^2 + (y_m - y_i)^2\}^{1/2}}\}, \quad (5.7)$$

$$\frac{\partial E}{\partial y_m} = \sum_{i \neq m} k_{mi} \{(y_m - y_i) - \frac{l_{mi}(y_m - y_i)}{\{(x_m - x_i)^2 + (y_m - y_i)^2\}^{1/2}}\}. \quad (5.8)$$

We must solve these $2n$ simultaneous non-linear equations of (5.6). But they cannot be directly solved by the $2n$-dimensional Newton-Raphson method, because they are not independent of one another, i.e.,

$$\sum_{m=1}^{n} \frac{\partial E}{\partial x_m} = 0, \quad \sum_{m=1}^{n} \frac{\partial E}{\partial y_m} = 0.$$

Then, we have adopted another way in which only one particle $p_m(x_m, y_m)$ is moved to its stable point at a time, freezing other particles. That is, viewing E as the function of only x_m and y_m, we compute a local minimum of E by the two-dimensional Newton-Raphson method. We can obtain a local minimum which satisfies (5.6) by iterating this step. In each step, we choose the particle that has the largest value of Δ_m, which is defined as

$$\Delta_m = \sqrt{\left\{ \frac{\partial E}{\partial x_m} \right\}^2 + \left\{ \frac{\partial E}{\partial y_m} \right\}^2}. \qquad (5.9)$$

The selected particle $p_m(x_m, y_m)$ is moved to the position which satisfies

$$\frac{\partial E}{\partial x_m} = \frac{\partial E}{\partial y_m} = 0.$$

Starting from $(x_m^{(0)}, y_m^{(0)})$ which is equal to the current position (x_m, y_m), the following step is iterated;

$$x_m^{(t+1)} = x_m^{(t)} + \delta x, \quad y_m^{(t+1)} = y_m^{(t)} + \delta y \quad \text{for } t = 0, 1, 2, \cdots . \quad (5.10)$$

The unknowns δx and δy satisfy a pair of linear equations as follows;

$$\frac{\partial^2 E}{\partial x_m^2}(x_m^{(t)}, y_m^{(t)}) \, \delta x + \frac{\partial^2 E}{\partial x_m \partial y_m}(x_m^{(t)}, y_m^{(t)}) \, \delta y = \frac{-\partial E}{\partial x_m}(x_m^{(t)}, y_m^{(t)}), \quad (5.11)$$

$$\frac{\partial^2 E}{\partial y_m \partial x_m}(x_m^{(t)}, y_m^{(t)}) \, \delta x + \frac{\partial^2 E}{\partial y_m^2}(x_m^{(t)}, y_m^{(t)}) \, \delta y = \frac{-\partial E}{\partial y_m}(x_m^{(t)}, y_m^{(t)}). \quad (5.12)$$

The coefficients of the above equations (5.11) and (5.12), which are the elements of Jacobian matrix, are computed from the partial derivatives of (5.7) and (5.8) by x_m and y_m as follows;

$$\frac{\partial^2 E}{\partial x_m^2} = \sum_{i \neq m} k_{mi} \left\{ 1 - \frac{l_{mi} (y_m - y_i)^2}{\{(x_m - x_i)^2 + (y_m - y_i)^2\}^{3/2}} \right\}, \qquad (5.13)$$

$$\frac{\partial^2 E}{\partial x_m \partial y_m} = \sum_{i \neq m} k_{mi} \frac{l_{mi} (x_m - x_i)(y_m - y_i)}{\{(x_m - x_i)^2 + (y_m - y_i)^2\}^{3/2}}, \qquad (5.14)$$

$$\frac{\partial^2 E}{\partial y_m \partial x_m} = \sum_{i \neq m} k_{mi} \frac{l_{mi}(x_m - x_i)(y_m - y_i)}{\{(x_m - x_i)^2 + (y_m - y_i)^2\}^{3/2}}, \qquad (5.15)$$

$$\frac{\partial^2 E}{\partial y_m^2} = \sum_{i \neq m} k_{mi} \{1 - \frac{l_{mi}(x_m - x_i)^2}{\{(x_m - x_i)^2 + (y_m - y_i)^2\}^{3/2}}\}. \qquad (5.16)$$

The unknowns δx and δy are computed from (5.11)-(5.16). The iteration (5.10) terminates when the value of Δ_m at $(x_m^{(t)}, y_m^{(t)})$ becomes enough small.

The global energy E is sure to converge to a local minimum if E is always decreased after the step of moving a particle. In order to guarantee the decrease of E, we test the value of E after the Newton-Raphson iteration, and retry the moving step by changing the starting derivatives if the new E is not smaller than the old.

Algorithm

In our graph drawing algorithm, first the distance d_{ij} must be computed for all pairs of vertices of a given graph. For the present, we are using a simple shortest path algorithm of Floyd [47]. Next l_{ij} and k_{ij} are computed for all pairs from d_{ij} by the use of (5.2), (5.3) and (5.4). Before starting the minimization process, we must determine the initial positions of particles. The experiments have shown that the initial positions do not have a great influence on the resultant pictures, except for the special cases: e.g., all particles lie on a single line. Now we are using a simple initialization method by which the particles are placed on the nodes of the regular n-polygon circumscribed by a circle whose diameter is L_0 (as for L_0, see (5.3)). After initializing the positions, the energy E is decreased, step by step, by moving a particle to a stable position.

The algorithm is summarized in a simple form as follows.

> compute d_{ij} for $1 \leq i \neq j \leq n$;
> compute l_{ij} for $1 \leq i \neq j \leq n$;
> compute k_{ij} for $1 \leq i \neq j \leq n$;
> initialize $p_1, p_2, ..., p_n$;
> while $(\max_i \Delta_i > \varepsilon)$ {
>
> >   let p_m be the particle satisfying $\Delta_m = \max_i \Delta_i$;
> >
> >   while $(\Delta_m > \varepsilon)$ {
> >
> > >   compute δx and δy by solving (5.11) and (5.12);
> > > $x_m := x_m + \delta x$;
> > > $y_m := y_m + \delta y$;
> >
> >   }
>
> }

Here we discuss the computational cost of the above algorithm briefly. As for d_{ij}, $O(n^3)$ time is required preliminarily.[1] Required computational time is mainly determined by the nested *while* loops. In the inner loop which is the Newton-Raphson iteration, $O(n)$ time is required to compute Δ_m and to compute δx and δy respectively at each step. In the outer loop, $O(n)$ time is required to compute the maximum of Δ_i because updating each Δ_i ($i \neq m$) after moving p_m can be performed in $O(1)$ time by memorizing the old position of p_m. As a result, the time needed to terminate the *while* loops is $O(T \cdot n)$ where T is the total number of inner loops. It is difficult to estimate T because T depends both on given graphs, especially the number of vertices (n), and on the initial positions of vertices. However, lowering the convergence precision (ε) is an effective way to reduce T.

---

[1] We can use instead more efficient shortest path algorithms [94, 121] for large graphs.

Figure 5.5 and 5.6 illustrate the process of minimizing E in the cases of two simple graphs. In Fig. 5.5, first particle F is moved (Fig. 5.5(b)) and next particle C is moved (Fig. 5.5(c)). The final state (Fig. 5.5(d)) is obtained after 20 moving steps. In Fig. 5.6, first particle B is moved (Fig. 5.6(b)) and next particle F is moved (Fig. 5.6(c)). The final state (Fig. 5.6(d)) is obtained after 21 moving steps.

Improvement by Exchanging Vertices

Though the algorithm proposed above does not guarantee to compute the true minimum of E, it seems to produce pretty satisfactory pictures as shown in the next section. Our goal is not to optimize the layouts at too much computational cost, but to get good layouts enough for human understanding at a reasonable cost. We here describe a simple method of improving the minimization process in order to produce much better pictures. After the local minimization, we try to do a test that we exchange the positions of a pair of particles and calculate the new energy for all pairs. If any one of energies thus calculated is smaller than the current local minimum, the energy minimization process is restarted from the corresponding state.

Figure 5.7 illustrates this process. Starting from the initial state (Fig. 5.7(a)), the energy converges to a local minimum (Fig. 5.7(b)). Then particles A and E are exchanged by performing this test (Fig. 5.7(c)). The energy minimization process is restarted from this state and finally the energy converges to the true minimum (Fig. 5.7(d)). By introducing this additional rule, the energy is considerably prevented from converging to a large local minimum.

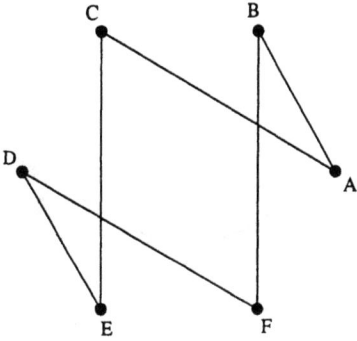

(a) initial state

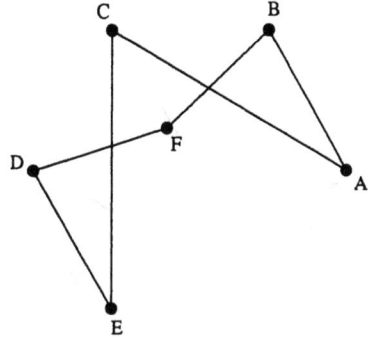

(b) first step

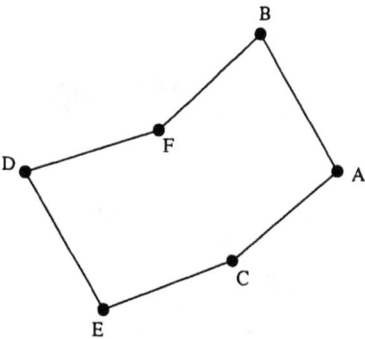

(c) second step

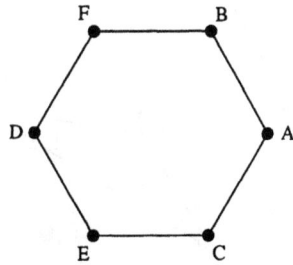

(d) final state

Figure 5.5: The energy minimization process (1).

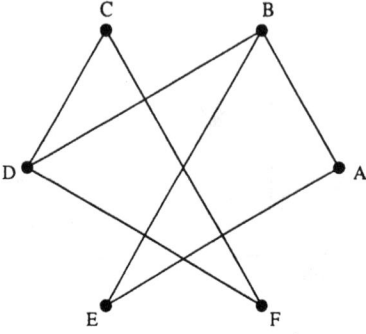

(a) initial state

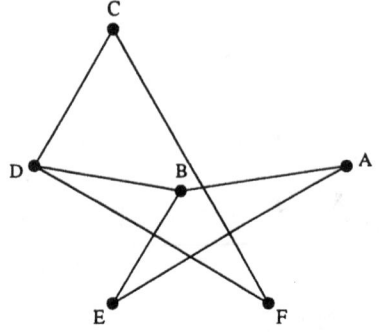

(b) first step

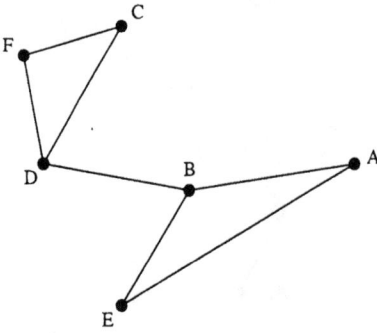

(c) second step

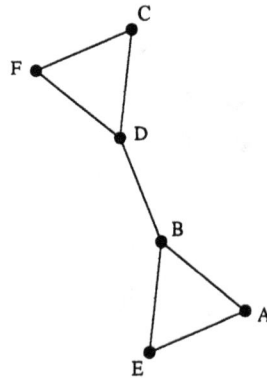

(d) final state

Figure 5.6:   The energy minimization process (2).

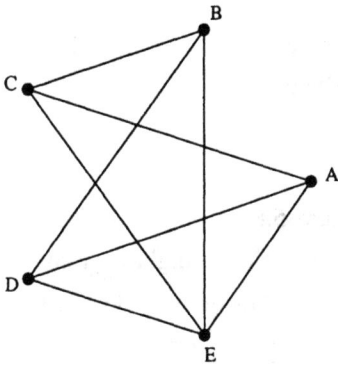

(a) initial state

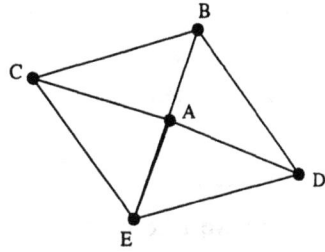

(b) local minimum

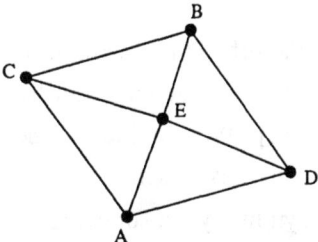

(c) exchange A and E

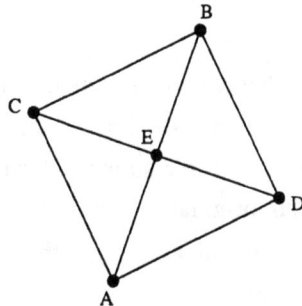

(d) final state

Figure 5.7: The energy minimization process by exchanging vertices.

5.3. Examples

We show some pictures of symmetric graphs, asymmetric graphs, isomorphic graphs, and weighted graphs. These pictures were generated by the
system implementing our graph drawing algorithm.

Symmetric Graphs

First we take up symmetric graphs. Figure 5.8 shows the pictures of
five regular polyhedron graphs as the typical examples of highly symmetric
graphs. Fig. 5.8(a)-5.8(e) are tetrahedron, cube, octahedron, dodecahedron,
and icosahedron respectively. They look as if they were the projected
images of actual three-dimensional regular polyhedrons. Figure 5.9 shows
the pictures of other symmetric graphs. Fig. 5.9(a) and 5.9(b) show the pictures of grid graphs. Fig. 5.9(c) shows the picture of the graph cited in Fig.
5.2. Fig. 5.9(d) shows the picture of a unitransitive graph. As these examples show, symmetries of graphs are visualized pleasingly as symmetric pictures in our system.

Detection of symmetry in general graphs is a difficult problem. In fact,
it is known that the problem of determining whether a given graph has a
fixed-point-free automorphism is NP-complete [82]. We can find symmetry
in an original graph from the generated picture, as described in [43].
Several efficient algorithms for detecting symmetry in drawings are
developed [40].

Asymmetric Graphs

Figure 5.10 shows the pictures of small asymmetric graphs, and Figure
5.11 shows the pictures of 20-vertex asymmetric graphs. In these cases, vertices and edges are distributed uniformly. Edges are almost of the same
length. Needless edge crossings are avoided to a great extent.

It can be said that our graph drawing algorithm is convincingly shown
to be practically useful by these symmetric and asymmetric pictures. The
CPU time needed to compute a layout in these pictures is listed in Table 5.1.

picture	vertices(n)	iterations(T)	CPU time (sec)
Fig. 5.8(a)	4	11	0.80
Fig. 5.8(b)	8	29	0.42
Fig. 5.8(c)	6	51	0.41
Fig. 5.8(d)	20	286	7.61
Fig. 5.8(e)	12	45	1.30
Fig. 5.9(a)	9	46	0.77
Fig. 5.9(b)	10	35	0.68
Fig. 5.9(c)	16	105	2.91
Fig. 5.9(d)	20	143	4.46
Fig. 5.10(a)	7	17	0.17
Fig. 5.10(b)	9	40	0.69
Fig. 5.10(c)	10	53	0.97
Fig. 5.10(d)	12	112	2.40
Fig. 5.11(a)	20	116	3.56
Fig. 5.11(b)	20	68	2.17
Fig. 5.11(c)	20	197	5.92
Fig. 5.11(d)	20	272	8.10

Table 5.1: The CPU time needed to compute a layout.

A layout is computed within 10 seconds on a VAX 8600. In our system, the labels of vertices are automatically placed at the appropriate positions according to the following strategy. The label of a vertex is positioned between the two adjacent edges going out from the vertex whose angle is the largest.

Isomorphic Graphs

When analyzing the structures of a model, it is a common practice to find out difference, likeness, and other relations by comparing some structures. Therefore the drawing system should produce the pictures of structures so that viewers can compare them easily. Here we take up isomorphism as one of the most basic relations between graphs. Isomorphic graphs which have the same internal structure are desired to be drawn as the same picture. Otherwise viewers cannot understand isomorphism from the pictures. Graph drawing algorithms should meet this requirement of congruity or uniqueness of generated pictures [122]. The problem of isomorphism determination of general graphs is an intractable problem, and all known algorithms have a running time exponential on the number of vertices in the worst case [34, 58, 93]. [2]

In our method, the stable states of the spring systems to which isomorphic graphs correspond can be thought the same though there may be more than one stable state. Therefore, isomorphic graphs are expected to be drawn as the same picture(s) by minimizing E. They are, in fact, drawn as the pictures one of which can be identified with the other by translating, rotating, and sometimes reflecting it. Figure 5.12 illustrates the pictures of a pair of isomorphic graphs. Fig. 5.12(a) and 5.12(b) show the pictures of initial state in our algorithm. It is difficult for viewers to detect isomorphism from these pictures. It is, however, pretty easy to find out isomorphism from the resultant pictures in Fig. 5.12(c) and 5.12(d). The CPU time needed to compute both layouts in Fig. 5.12(c) and 5.12(d) is about 2 seconds on a VAX 8600. On the other hand, it takes about 18 minutes CPU time to solve this isomorphism problem combinatorially by a naive thorough search. This "drawing" approach can be said to be a good approximate method for graph isomorphism, though the pictures of isomorphic graphs can not always be regarded as identical because the total spring energy does not always converge to the same minimum in our algorithm. The judgement of isomorphism from the resultant pictures could be done automatically by making use of the geometric attributes yielded by the drawing system.

---

[2] It is known that subgraph isomorphism problem is NP-complete. However, graph isomorphism problem remains open for both directed and undirected graphs [51].

In addition, our algorithm brings the satisfactory results as for the "like-ness" of graphs. The graphs which have a small difference are desired to be drawn as the pictures which have a small difference. Figure 5.13 shows the pictures of two graphs similar to the graph in Fig. 5.12(a). The only differ-ence between Fig. 5.12(a) and 5.13(a) is the existence of edge DJ, and the difference between Fig. 5.12(a) and 5.13(b) is the existence of vertex K and edges KA and KE. These differences can be understood by glancing at the pictures.

Weighted Graphs

In order to model practical problems, we often use weighted graphs in which "weights" are associated with edges. For example, in a transport model in which vertices and edges represent cities and routes respectively, weights might represent the distances or costs between cities. If we can visualize weighted graphs by regarding weights as geometric distances in the drawings, we may understand the overall structures of them graphically.

We apply our graph drawing algorithm to weighted graphs straightfor-wardly. In a weighted graph, the distance between vertices is defined as the summation of weights. Then, we relate the distance in a weighted graph to the desirable distance in the drawing. Figure 5.14 shows the pictures of two weighted graphs generated by our system. The overall images regarding weights can be understood intuitively from these pictures.

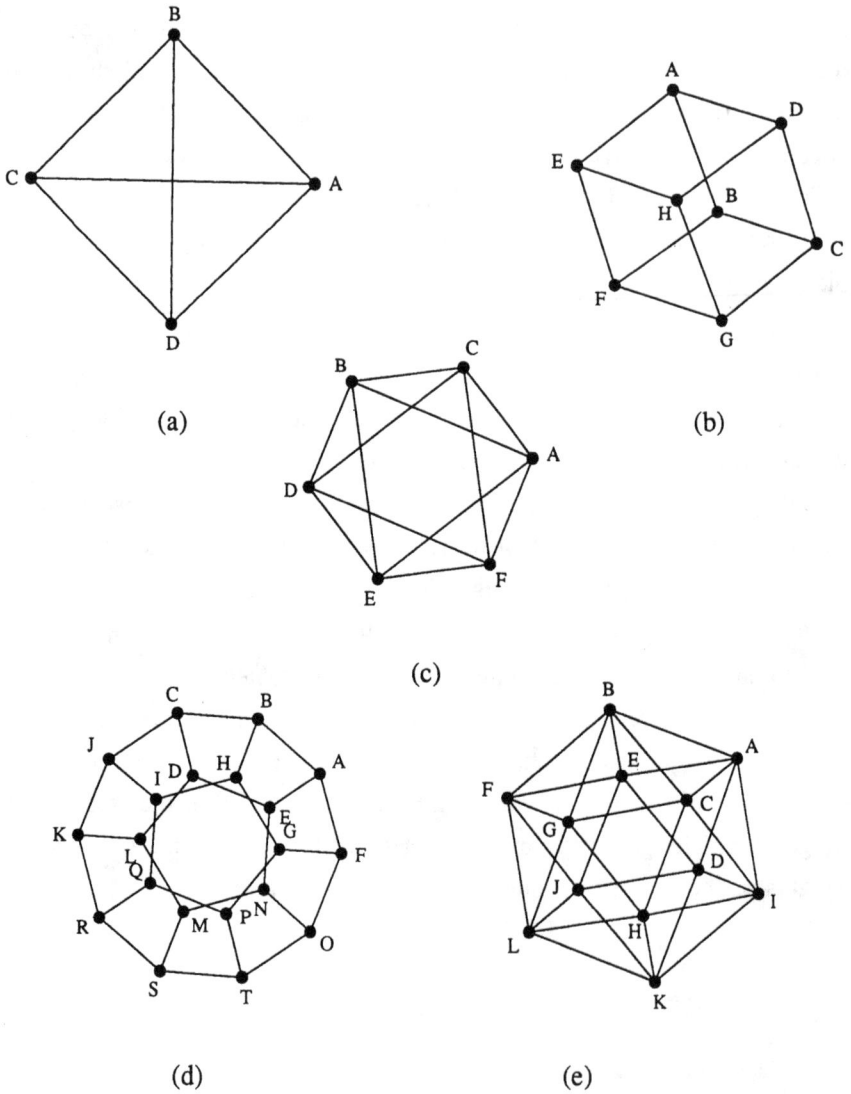

Figure 5.8: Pictures of regular polyhedron graphs.

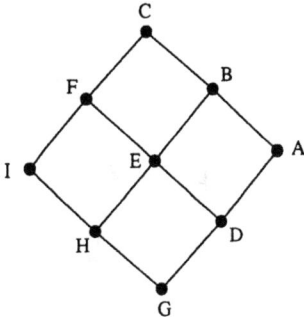

(a)

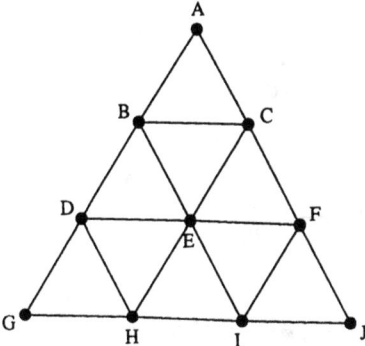

(b)

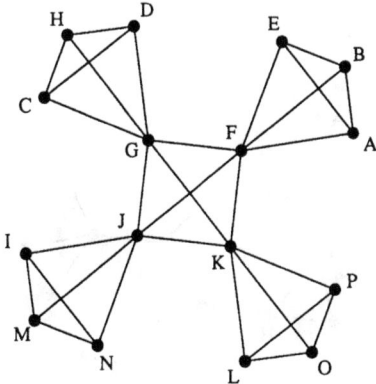

(c)

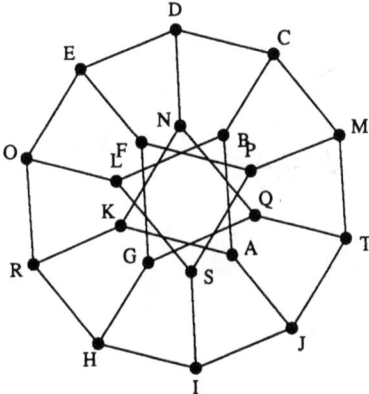

(d)

Figure 5.9: Pictures of symmetric graphs.

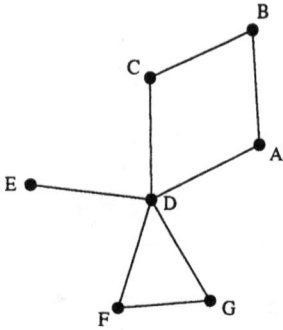

(a)

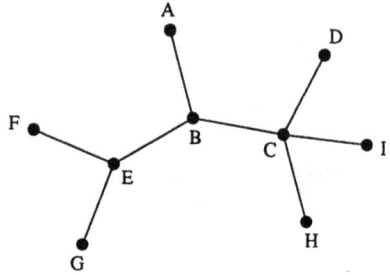

(b)

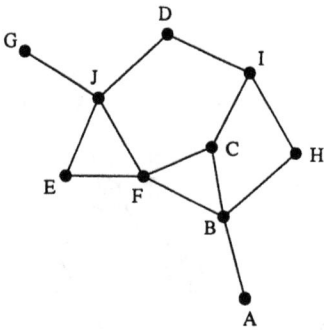

(c)

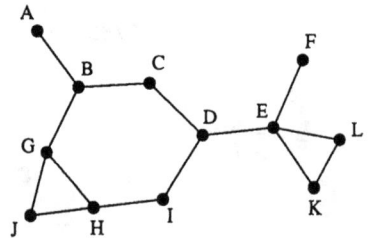

(d)

Figure 5.10:   Pictures of asymmetric graphs.

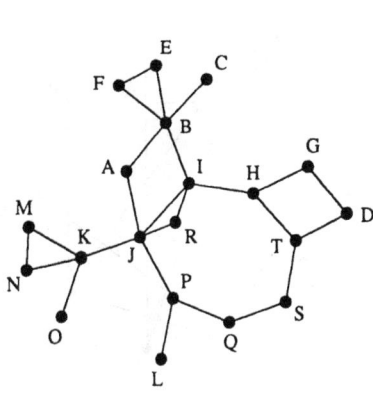

(a)

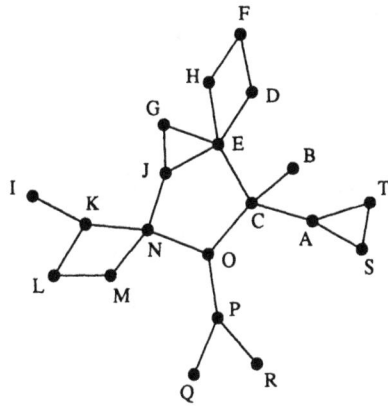

(b)

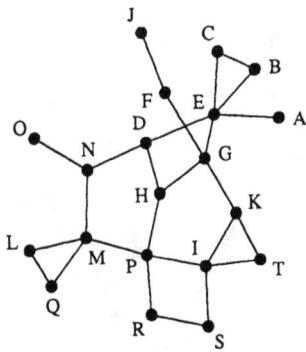

(c)

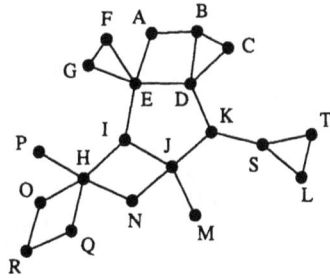

(d)

Figure 5.11: Pictures of 20-vertex asymmetric graphs.

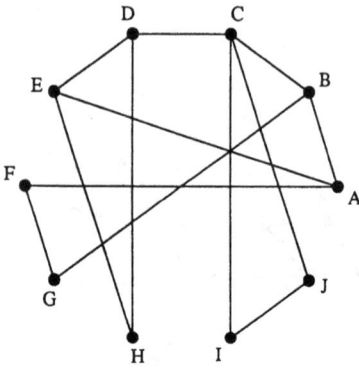

(a) initial state of graph 1

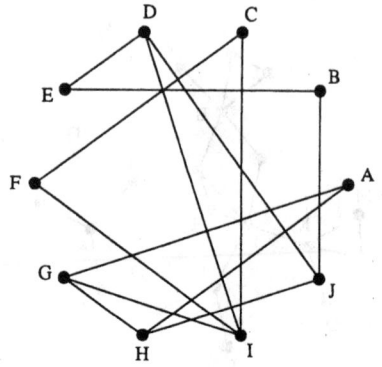

(b) initial state of graph 2

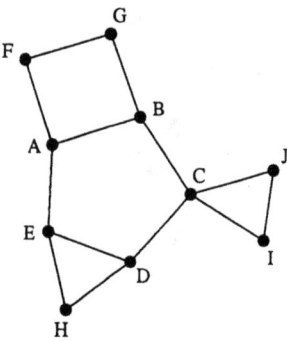

(c) final state of graph 1

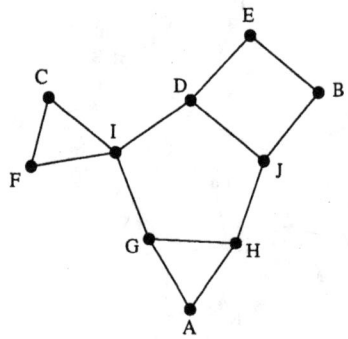

(d) final state of graph 2

Figure 5.12: Pictures of isomorphic graphs.

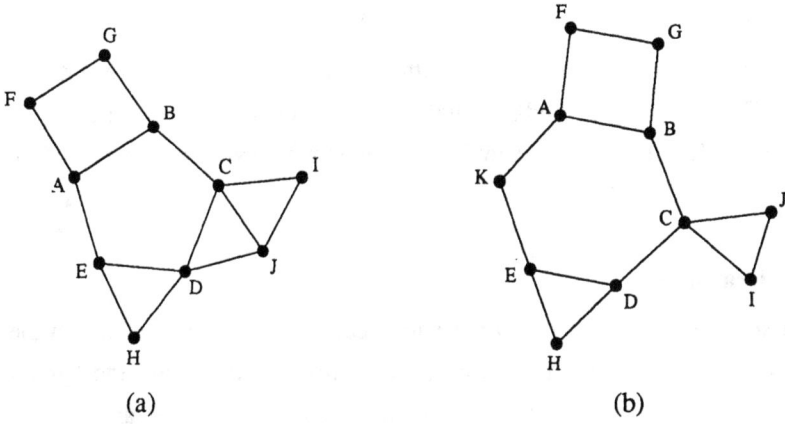

Figure 5.13:   Pictures of the graphs similar to the graph in Fig. 5.12(a).

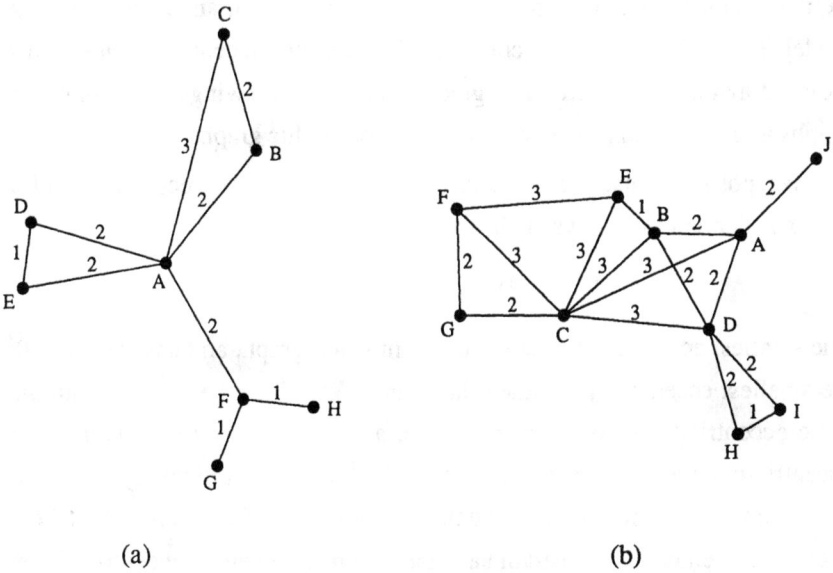

Figure 5.14:   Pictures of weighted graphs.

5.4. Application to Radial Drawings and Layered Drawings

In our original spring algorithm, the positions of vertices are not restricted. We apply the method to radial drawings in which vertices are placed
on concentric circles and to layered drawings in which vertices are placed on
parallel lines.

Radial Drawings

In some applications, radial or centrifugal graph drawings in which the
vertices of each level are placed on a concentric circle around the "graph
theoretic" center are useful to understand the overall relations among elements. Radial drawing algorithms are investigated for undirected graphs
[27] and for free trees [15, 87]. Ring diagrams for visualizing hierarchies
are proposed in [108]. A method for drawing graphs which tries to minimize the circular dilation is proposed in [86]. We present an extended spring
model in which vertices are constrained to lie on concentric circles. This
radial drawing algorithm also gives symmetric drawings of symmetric
graphs and almost congruent drawings of isomorphic graphs.

We positively use the "eccentricity" of vertices. The eccentricity of a
vertex is defined as follows [11];

$$e(v_i) = \max_{j \neq i} d_{ij}. \qquad (5.17)$$

The smallest eccentricity is called the radius of a graph, and any vertex with
the smallest eccentricity is called the center. We place the vertices with the
same eccentricity on a concentric circle, and place the vertices with larger
eccentricity on a larger circle like the method in [27]. Particularly the graph
theoretic center is placed at the center of the concentric circles, when there
is only one center. To constrain each particle p_i to lie on a concentric circle,
we express the position of each particle as follows;

$$p_i = (r_i \cos\theta_i, r_i \sin\theta_i). \qquad (5.18)$$

The radius r_i is determined by the use of the eccentricity $e(v_i)$. The

determination procedure is divided into three cases depending on the
number of graph theoretic centers (C) as follows;

$$
r_i = \begin{cases}
L \times (e(v_i) - rad) & \text{for } |C| = 1, \\
L \times (e(v_i) - rad + 1/2) & \text{for } |C| = 2, \\
L \times (e(v_i) - rad + 1) & \text{for } |C| \geq 3,
\end{cases}
\tag{5.19}
$$

where L is the same constant as the one in (5.2) and rad is the graph
theoretic radius. Then, we rewrite (5.1) as the function of $\theta_1, \theta_2, ..., \theta_n$ as
follows;

$$
E = \sum_{i=1}^{n-1} \sum_{j=i+1}^{n} \frac{1}{2} k_{ij} \{ r_i^2 + r_j^2 - 2r_i r_j \cos(\theta_i - \theta_j) + l_{ij}^2 \tag{5.20}
$$
$$
- 2l_{ij} \sqrt{r_i^2 + r_j^2 - 2r_i r_j \cos(\theta_i - \theta_j)} \}.
$$

We compute a local minimum of E from an initial state based on the
Newton-Raphson iteration like our original spring algorithm. We are using
a simple initialization by which the particles of each level are placed on each
circle at equal intervals. In addition, we introduce a test by which the positions of a pair of particles are exchanged and the energy E is calculated. We
can improve the initial layout by doing this test for some pairs before the
energy minimization process. Figure 5.15 illustrates the process of minimizing E. In the first four steps, the particles I, J, D, and H are moved to their
stable positions (Fig. 5.15(b)-(e)). The final layout is obtained after about
140 steps (Fig. 5.15(f)).

Figure 5.16 and 5.17 show the resultant radial drawings. In Fig. 5.16,
symmetric structures are visualized as radial symmetric pictures pleasingly.
Fig. 5.17 shows the radial drawings of 20-vertex asymmetric graphs which
appeared in Fig. 5.11. In these cases, needless edge crossings are avoided to
a great extent. Though the method is not effective for a kind of graphs
whose vertices have the same eccentricity such as regular polyhedron
graphs, it can be widely used for drawing other kinds of graphs, especially
free trees.

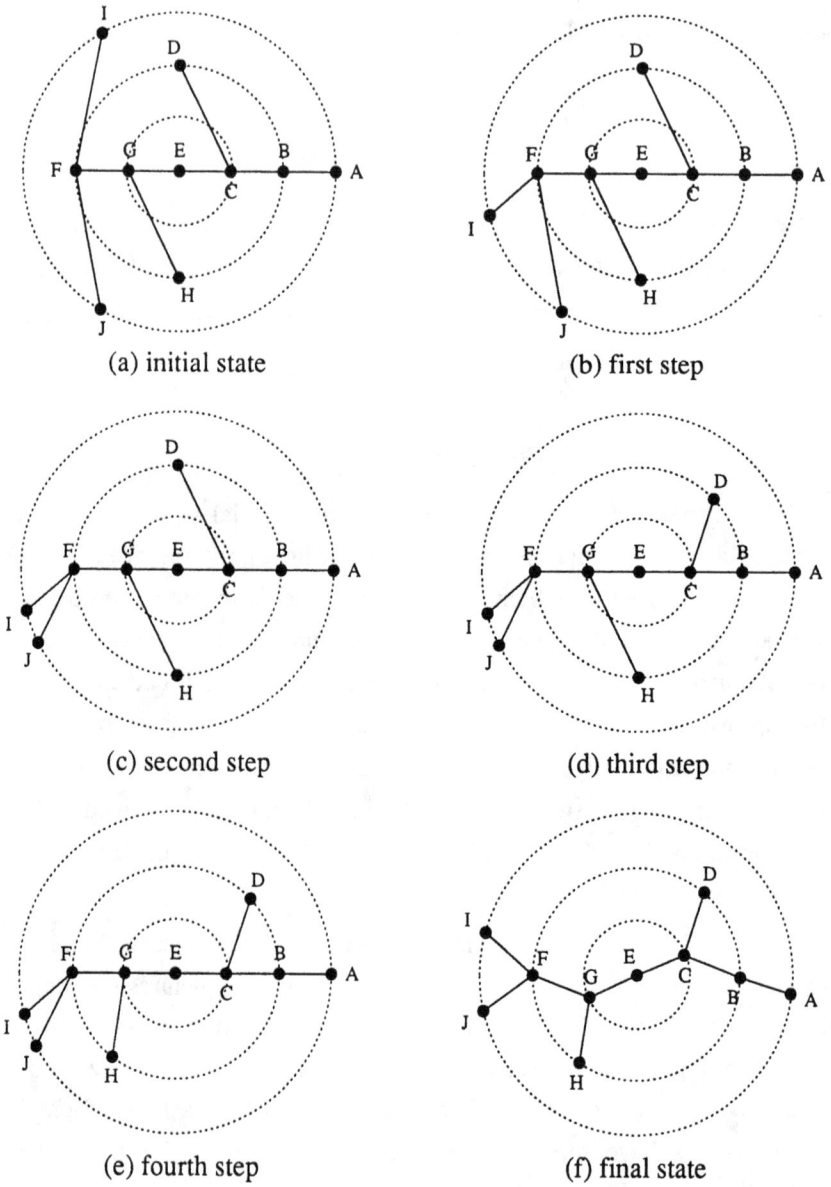

(a) initial state

(b) first step

(c) second step

(d) third step

(e) fourth step

(f) final state

Figure 5.15:   Radial layout process.

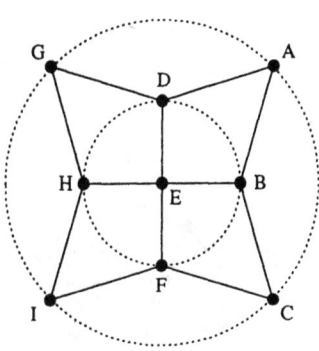

(a)

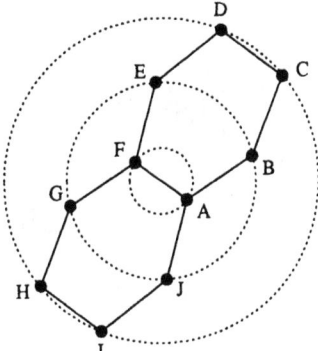

(b)

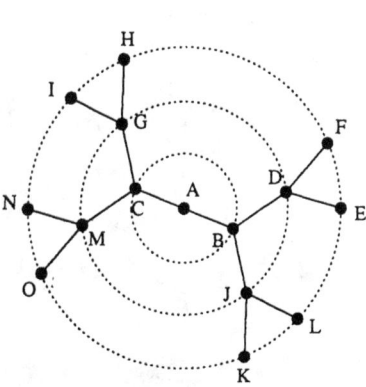

(c)

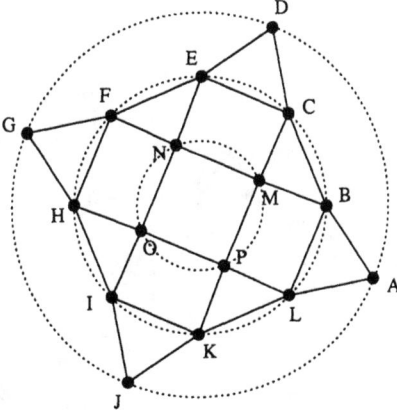

(d)

Figure 5.16: Radial drawings of symmetric graphs.

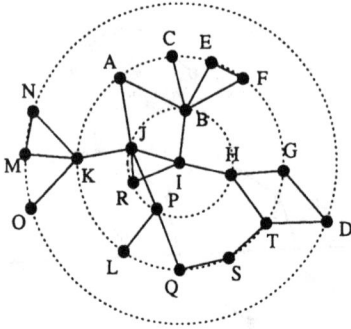

(a)

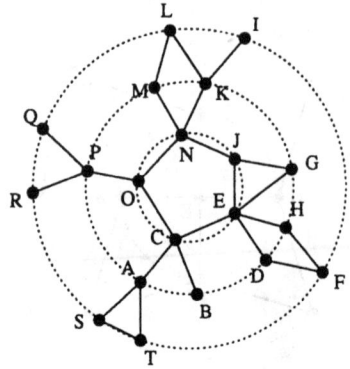

(b)

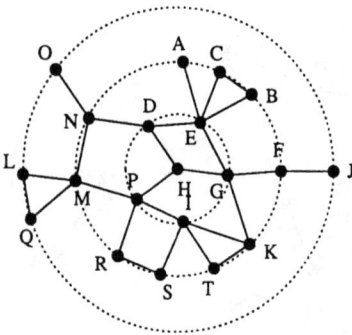

(c)

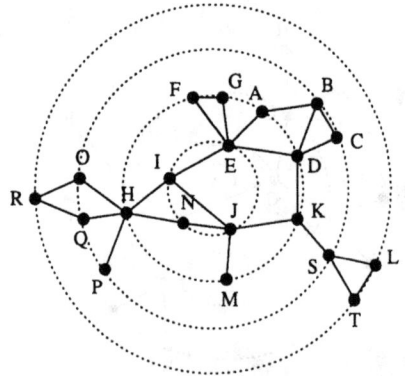

(d)

Figure 5.17:   Radial drawings of asymmertic graphs.

Layered Drawings

Acyclic digraphs are commonly used to visualize hierarchies. A layered or hierarchical drawing of an acyclic digraph is an upward (a downward) drawing in which the vertices of each hierarchy level are placed on a horizontal line. Hierarchical drawings are investigated in [27, 92, 112, 124]. We apply our spring algorithm to layered drawings. This layered drawing algorithm also inherits the symmetric drawing property from the original algorithm.

First we assign the hierarchy level to each vertex. In some cases, the assignment is given. In other cases, the hierarchy level $l(v_i)$ of a vertex v_i is defined as the maximum number of edges of any path terminating at v_i. To constrain each particle p_i to lie on a horizontal line, we express the position of it as follows;

$$p_i = (x_i, L \times l(v_i)) \tag{5.21}$$

where L is the same constant as the one in (5.2). Then, we compute the values of $x_1, x_2, ..., x_n$ that minimize E. We can solve this problem as a special case of minimizing E in (5.5), in which $y_1, y_2, ..., y_n$ are fixed.

In the method, edge crossings can be avoided to some extent. The problem of minimizing the number of edge crossings for layered graphs is NP-complete, even if there are only two layers and the positions of the vertices on the second layer are fixed [42]. Figure 5.18 illustrates the initial state and the final state of our layout process for a 2-layered graph which is quoted from [41]. In this case, the reduction of edge crossings is optimized. The precise proof of this property is left as future work. Figure 5.19 shows the resultant layered drawings. In these examples, symmetric structures are visualized as layered symmetric pictures pleasingly.

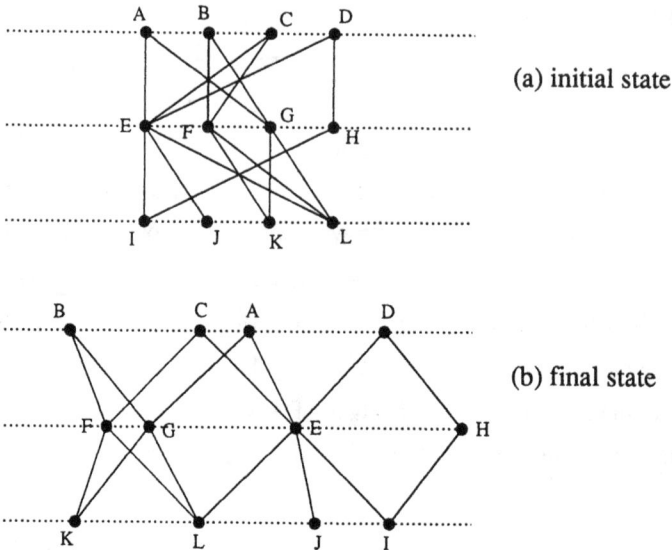

(a) initial state

(b) final state

Figure 5.18:   Reduction of eade crossings in a 2-layered graph.

5.5. Summary

We have proposed a method of drawing general undirected graphs for human understanding. It can be widely used in the information systems which deal with network structures. Our idea is quite simple and intuitive; the graph theoretic distance between vertices in a graph is related to the geometric distance between them in the drawing. As described above, our spring algorithm has many good properties; symmetric drawings of symmetric graphs, and almost congruent drawings of isomorphic graphs, uniform distribution of vertices, and a relatively small number of edge crossings. We have also taken up symmetry detection and isomorphism detection in graphs. These problems are too tough even for high-performance computers to solve in a combinatorial approach. The drawing approach for these difficult problems might be an interesting and promising research target.

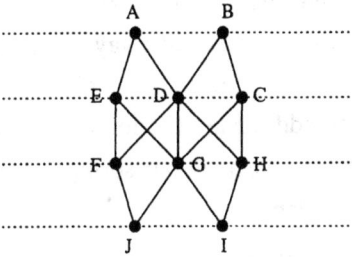

(a)

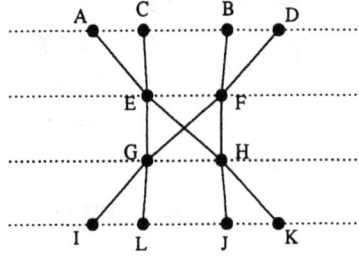

(b)

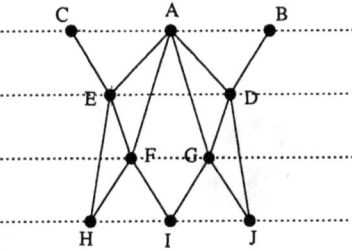

(c)

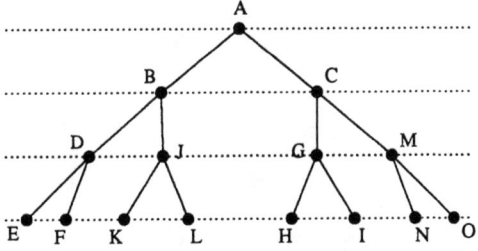

(d)

Figure 5.19: Layered drawings of symmetric graphs.

We have extended our spring algorithm to the algorithms for producing radial drawings of undirected graphs and layered drawings of acyclic digraphs. These algorithms inherit the good properties from the original method. The study of other variations of a "constrained" version by which the positions of vertices are geometrically constrained is underway. Though general digraphs can be drawn in the same way by neglecting the directions of edges, it may be necessary to introduce an additional criterion as for the directions of edges. It is a challenging research to extend our spring model in order to handle a variety of graph layout problems.

Our algorithm is suitable for dynamic graph drawing systems whose users can edit a graph interactively by inserting and deleting vertices and edges. A new layout of a modified graph can be obtained by restarting the energy minimization process from the modified state. A new pleasing drawing is expected to be near the old drawing. We are going to develop a browser for graph structures based on our spring model.

CHAPTER 6

APPLICATIONS

In this chapter, we present five applications of TRIP. First we take up the problem of visualizing relations expressed by English sentences. Since a natural language is of course the most intimate textual representation for us, the translation from natural language representations into pictorial representations is of great importance. We show two examples of translating English sentences into pictures, one of which is a graphics interface through natural language, and the other is the visualization of pedigree relationships. Next we take up the visualization of list structures as a typical problem of displaying data structures. Then we try to generate Nassi-Shneiderman diagrams from source programs written in some programming languages. Finally we challenge the problem of generating entity-relationship diagrams as a visualization problem in the area of databases.

6.1. A Graphics Interface through Natural Language

As an application of TRIP, we present a small prototype in which a picture is generated from the layout specification written in English. English sentences describe graphical objects, and positional or connectional relations among them. This system can be viewed as a plain English interface for COOL. For example, the following three sentences express a simple graphical layout;

> *(s1) Box1 and box2 are boxes.*
> *(s2) Box2 is placed on the right of box1.*
> *(s3) Box1 is connected to box2 by a line.*

The system reads these sentences and outputs the following picture.

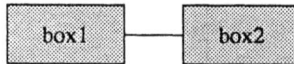

In this system, semantic relations of English sentences are mapped to graphical relations, then being visualized. We represent semantic relations as case structures based on the case grammar framework [110,144]. In this framework, the verb plays a central role in determining the structure of a sentence. Semantic or deep cases describe relationships between the verb and the constituents without regard to where they appear in surface structure. For the present, we are using the following set of cases, which is enough to deal with restricted sentences appeared in this section.

> Agent (ag)   --- instigator of the action
> Object (obj)   --- entity which is acted on
> Location (loc)   --- location or orientation of the event
> Goal (goal)   --- place which something is acted to
> Participant (part) --- entity which is involved
> Complement (comp)   --- complement

The vocabulary used in this small version is listed together with sample sentences in Figure 6.1. We use a special parser[1] in TRIP which translates a sentence into the underlying case structure. The above sentences (s1), (s2)

---

[1] This parser was originally implemented in Franz Lisp by Nobuo Satake. It is based on active chart parsing. The amount of time taken to parse a sentence is known to depend on the cube of its length if the grammar is ambiguous and the square of the length otherwise [144].

(a) Verbs

be	(ex.) X, Y, and Z are large boxes.
place	(ex.) X is placed on the left of Y.
put	(ex.) X is put on Y.
lay	(ex.) X and Y are laid below Z.
lie	(ex.) X lies above Y and Z.
contain	(ex.) X contains Y. Y is contained by X.
hide	(ex.) X hides Y. Y is hidden by X.
connect	(ex.) X is connected to Y by a solid line.
arrange	(ex.) X, Y, and Z are arranged horizontally.

(b) Prepositions

on the left of	(ex.) X lies on the left of Y.
on the right of	(ex.) Y lies on the right of X.
above	(ex.) X and Y are placed above Z.
below	(ex.) Put X below Y.
on	(ex.) X is placed on Y.
under	(ex.) X is laid under Y.
between	(ex.) X is placed between Y and Z.
with	(ex.) X is put above Y with a connecting line.

(c) Adjectives and adverbs
   large, small, standard   (very large, very small)
   thick, thin, solid, dashed, dotted
   connecting
   white, black
   horizontally, vertically

Figure 6.1: The vocabulary of current English interface.

and (s3) are translated into their semantic structures in the form of Prolog predicates, as follows;

(r1) semantics([be, [present],
          ag(and([[box1, singular], [box2, singular]])),
          comp([box], plural])]).

(r2) semantics([place, [passive, present],
          ag([ ]),
          obj([box2, singular]),
          loc(on([right, def-arti, relation(of([box1, singular]))),
                          singular])))]).

(r3) semantics([connect, [passive, present],
  ag([line, indef-arti, singular]),
  obj([box1, singular]),
  goal(to([box2, singular])))]).

Note that a pair of corresponding active and passive sentences have the identical case structure.

Now we visualize semantic structures by mapping specific patterns of case relations to specific geometric or drawing relations. The above semantic structures are processed as follows. As for the verb *be*, its agent is mapped to the corresponding graphical object(s) depending on the complement case. As for the verb *place*, the relation between the object case and the location case is mapped to the corresponding geometric relation(s) depending on the preposition in the location case. As for the verb *connect*, the relation between the object case and the goal case is mapped to line connection(s). As a result, the semantic structures (r1), (r2) and (r3) are translated into the following visual structures;

(v1) boxwithlabel(box1, 60, 30, box1, [ ]),
  boxwithlabel(box2, 60, 30, box2, [ ]).
(v2) horizontallisting([box1, box2], 30, [ ]).
(v3) multi_connect([box1], [box2], center, center, [ ]).

COOL generated the above picture from the layout specification (v1), (v2) and (v3). Since it is slightly larger, the whole visual mapping of this application is listed in Appendix.

Figure 6.2 illustrates the pictures generated by this system. Several adjectives which describe the properties of objects and lines are interpreted by the system. A larger example is shown in Figure 6.3. The diagram in this figure represents the case structure of the sentence: BOX1 IS CON-NECTED TO BOX2 AND BOX3 BY SOLID LINES. The upper-case words in the sentences are regarded as nouns. The layout is specified by twenty-two sentences (182 words).

(a) Box1, box2, box3, and box4 are boxes.
     Box1 is placed on the left of box2.
     Box3 is laid below box1.
     Box2 lies above box4.
     Box1 is connected to box2 and box3
     by thick dashed lines.
     Solid lines connect box2 and box3 to box4.

(b) C1, c2, c3, c4, c5, c6, and c7 are very small
     circles.
     C1 is put above c2 and c3 with connecting lines.
     C2 is put above c4 and c5 with connecting lines.
     C3 is put above c6 and c7 with connecting lines.
     C4, c5, c6, and c7 are arranged horizontally.

(c) Box1 is a very large box.
     Box2 and box3 are standard white boxes.
     Box1 contains box2 and box3.
     Box1 is hidden by box2 and box3.

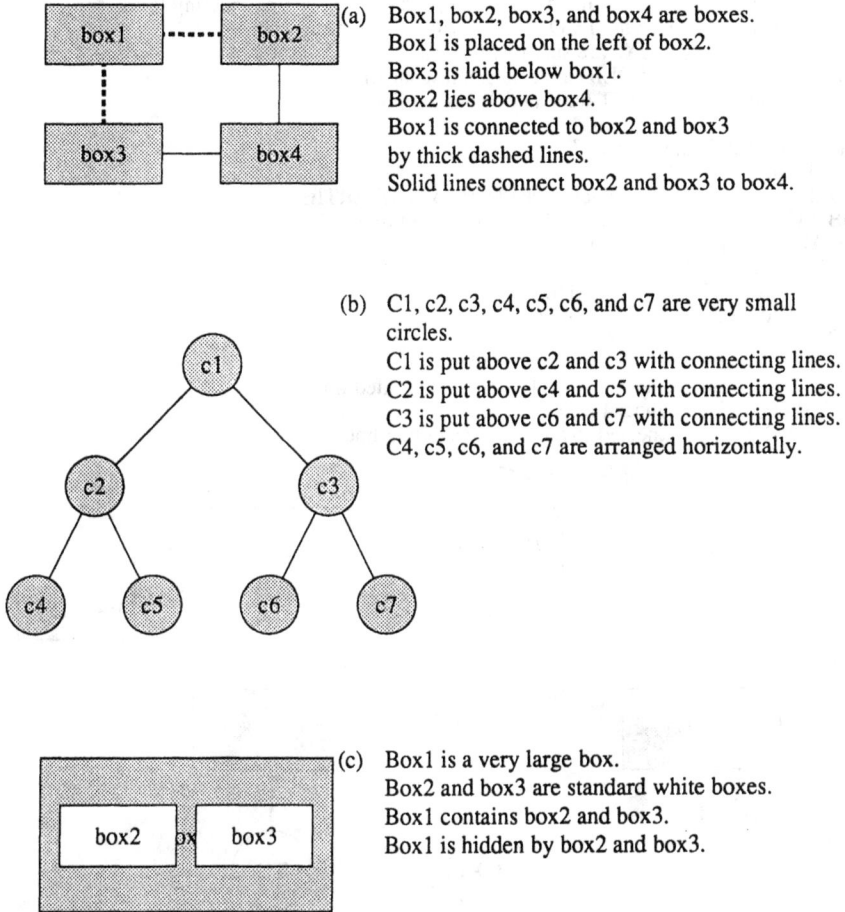

Figure 6.2: Pictures specified by English sentences.

CONNECT is a large white circle.
AGENT, OBJECT, GOAL, and STYLE are large boxes.
AGENT, OBJECT, and GOAL are arranged horizontally.
CONNECT is put above AGENT, OBJECT, and GOAL with connecting lines.
STYLE is put on the right of CONNECT with a connecting line.
BOX1, BOX2, and BOX3 are small white circles.
LINE, AND, TO, and SOLID are also small white circles.
LINE is put below AGENT with a thick dashed line.
PROPERTIES is a large box.
PROPERTIES is put below LINE with a line.
SOLID lies below PROPERTIES.
SOLID is connected by a thick dashed line to PROPERTIES.
OBJECT is put above BOX1 with a thick dashed line.
GOAL is put above TO with a thick dashed line.
AND is placed below TO.
BOX2 and BOX3 lie below AND.
AND is connected to BOX2, BOX3, and TO by lines.
BOX2 is laid on the left of BOX3.
PRESENT and PASSIVE are white standard boxes.
PRESENT is put on the right of STYLE with a dotted line.
PASSIVE is placed under PRESENT.
PASSIVE is also connected to STYLE by a dotted line.

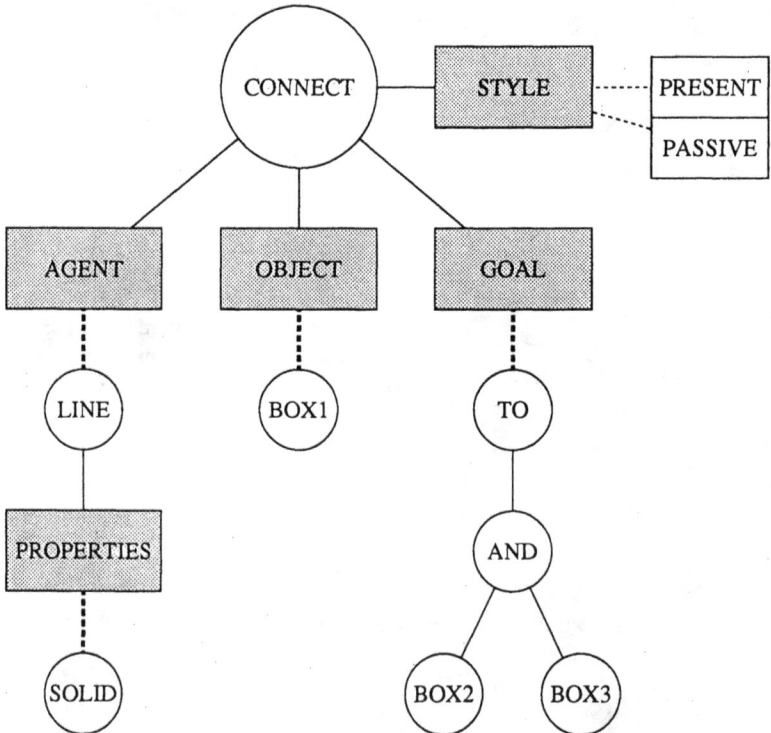

Figure 6.3: A diagram specified by twenty-two sentences.

We can build a real natural language interface for generating pictures by extending this approach. The main task for extension is to increase the vocabulary and add the mapping rules for new words. This growing process is similar to the one in the case of natural language translation systems. The system would be much more sophisticated by integrating up-to-date theories and techniques in natural language processing, such as situational semantics. Further, a natural language interface would become more and more powerful if it could be combined with a voice recognition system. A time will come in the near future when we can get a picture only by speaking to the computer as asking a friend.

6.2. Pedigree Charts

Here we describe an application in which pedigree (family) relationships described in English are translated into conventional pedigree charts. This application is a good example which uses pliable constraints. We use the same parser that is used in the previous section. We explain the translation process by giving an example. The input sentences are given as follows;

> *B is the wife of A.*
> *C, D, and E are the children of A.*
> *D is the husband of H.*
> *I and J are the children of H.*
> *E is the father of G.*
> *F is the mother of G.*

Several expressions are allowed to represent the relations among husband, wife and child (children), though the vocabulary is limited. The above sentences represent three families each of which consists of parents and a child or children. These sentences are first translated into their semantic structures as described before. The family relations are inferred from these semantics. The inference rules are specified as the definition of *family* predicate, which is listed in Appendix. Then, we can regard the relational structure as the following family relations;

> % family(Father, Mother, Children).
> family('A', 'B', ['C', 'D', 'E']).
> family('D', 'H', ['I', 'J']).
> family('E', 'F', ['G']).
> person('A').
> person('B').
> person('C').
> person('D').
> person('E').
> person('F').
> person('G').
> person('H').
> person('I').
> person('J').

The knowledge manipulation like this should be realized in the analyzing stage, though it is done as a part of visual mapping in this example. In any case, a method of representing and manipulating knowledge plays an important role in the visualization of knowledge.

We visualize the pedigree relationships by using the visual mapping in Figure 6.4. An object expressed by *person* is mapped to a box bounding its name (see *objectmap* in Fig. 6.4). As for relation mapping (see *relation-map* in Fig. 6.4), first two boxes corresponding to father and mother are arranged horizontally with a thick dotted connecting line. Next these boxes are placed above the boxes corresponding to a child or children, being connected to each child by a thin solid line. Finally x-coordinate constraints between children (see *hor_relation* in Fig. 6.4) are divided into four cases depending on whether a child is married or not. Such a distinction is necessary because we represent both the relation between parents and the relation between children as x-coordinate constraints. Note that y-coordinate constraints between parents and children and x-coordinate constraints between children are specified as pliable.

Figure 6.5(a) shows the resultant picture. In this case, pliable constraints are satisfied exactly. We add one more family to the above data;

K is the child of J.

G is the mother of K.

Now x-coordinate constraints become over-constrained. Fig. 6.5(b) shows the picture generated by computing the least square solution. Further we add one more family;

L and M are the children of C.

C is the husband of I.

The new relations[2] break the exact satisfaction of y-coordinate constraints besides x-coordinate ones. Fig. 6.5(c) shows the updated picture. To generate this picture, 99 rigid constraints and 13 pliable constraints among 108 variables are solved. As these pictures show, pleasing charts are obtained even when the pedigree relationships form a network structure. However, there may be more complicated cases that the visual mapping in this example cannot handle. In such cases, a more elaborate visual mapping including exchanges of the positions of children might be necessary.

It is difficult for us to understand the pedigree relationships from the original sentences. We must read them several times and may imagine the chart of them. A pictorial representation is so powerful that we can understand the overall structure by glancing at it. It can be said, therefore, that the knowledge visualization like this application is very useful for the user interface of knowledge manipulation systems.

---

[2] The pair *C* and *I* have the third degree of kinship, so they are prohibited legally from getting married now in Japan.

```
objectmap :-
      person( X ),
      boxwithlabel( X, 40, 20, X, [visible] ),
      fail.
```

```
relationmap :-
      family( F, M, C ),
      % relation between father and mother
      point( [F, M] ),
      horizontallisting( [F, [F, M], M], 20, [rigid] ),
      connect( F, M, right, left, [thick, dotted] ),
      % relation between parents and children
      x_average( [F, M], C, [rigid] ),
      ver_map( [F, M], C ),
      % relation among children
      hor_map( C ),
      fail.
```

```
ver_map( _, [] ).
ver_map( P, [C | L] ) :-
      y_order( [P, C], 50, [pliable] ),
      connect( P, C, bottom, top, [orthogonal, thin, solid] ),
      ver_map( P, L ).
```

```
hor_map( [_] ).
hor_map( [X, Y | L] ) :-
      hor_relation( X, Y ), hor_map( [Y | L] ).
```

```
hor_relation( X, Y ) :-
      family( X, W, _ ),
      family( H, Y, _ ), !,
      x_order( [W, H], 40, [pliable] ).
```

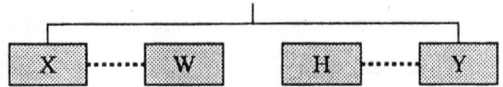

```
hor_relation( X, Y ) :-
      family( X, W, _ ), !,
      x_order( [W, Y], 40, [pliable] ).
```

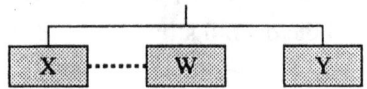

```
hor_relation( X, Y ) :-
      family( H, Y, _ ), !,
      x_order( [X, H], 40, [pliable] ).
```

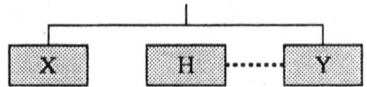

```
hor_relation( X, Y ) :-
      x_order( [X, Y], 40, [pliable] ).
```

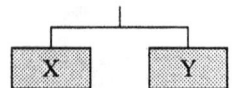

Figure 6.4:   Visual mapping for pedigree charts.

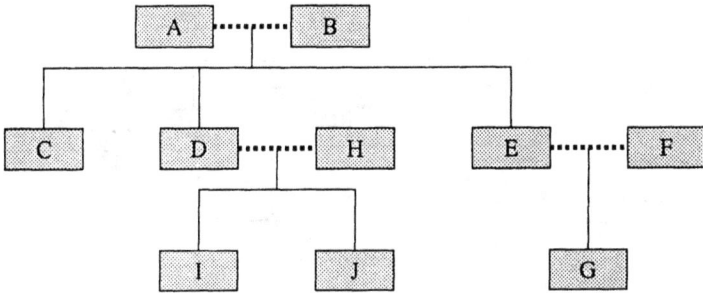

(a) All constraints are satisfied exactly.

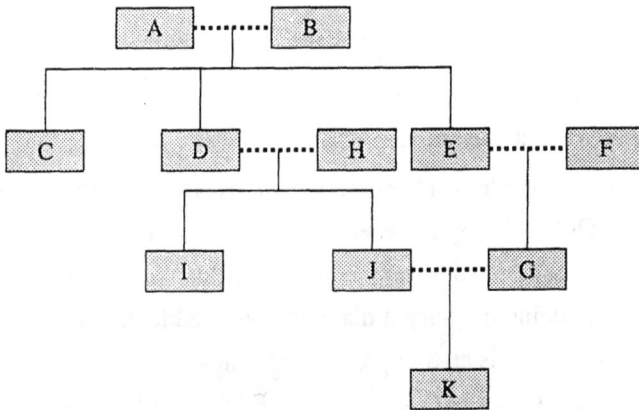

(b) X-coordinate constraints are conflicting.

Figure 6.5: Pedigree charts.

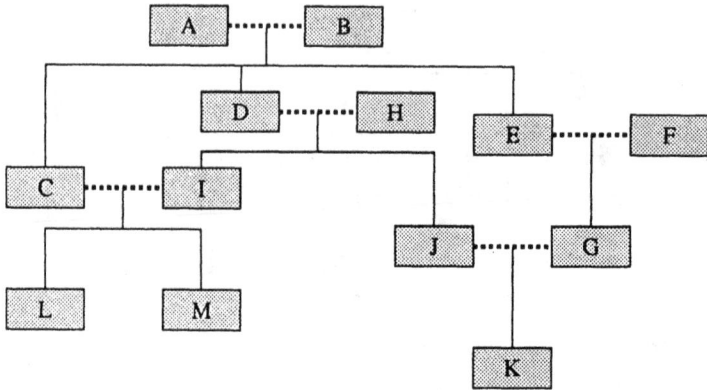

(c) Both x-coordinate constraints and y-coordinate constraints
   are conflicting.

Figure 6.5:   Pedigree charts (continued).

6.3. Diagrams for List Structures

We present a simple application which uses the picture hierarchy
mechanism of COOL. We try to generate diagrams for illustrating list structures that may be found in some textbooks of LISP language. A list is visualized as cells and pointers. Such a diagram was used to animate LISP programs in [37]. The input is an S-expression as follows;

$$((A (B)) (((C) D) (E) F) (G H)).$$

Since it is the *cons* structure of a given list that we want to visualize, we
translate the original data into the relational structure representing the *cons*
structure explicitly. By a simple parser, the above data is translated into the
following predicate;

cons(cons('A', cons(cons('B', nil), nil)), cons(cons(cons(cons('C', nil),
cons('D', nil)), cons(cons('E', nil), cons('F', nil))),
cons(cons('G', cons('H', nil)), nil))).

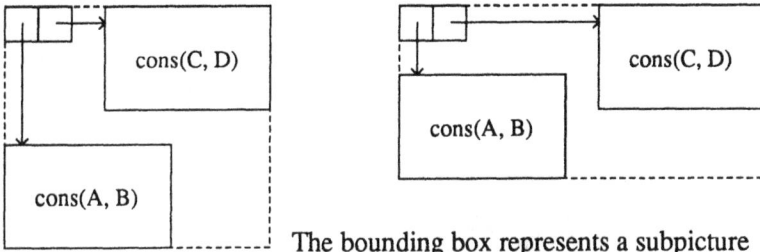

The bounding box represents a subpicture corresponding to cons(cons(A, B), cons(C, D)).

(a) vertical type composition   (b) horizontal type composition

Figure 6.6: Composite rules of cells.

Now we concentrate on visualizing this hierarchical relational structure. We map each *cons* (X, Y) pattern to a subpicture which includes a cell. If X or Y is also a *cons* pattern, it is mapped to a subordinate subpicture. In this case, the subpicture corresponding to the car-part is placed below the cell, and the one corresponding to the cdr-part is placed on the right of it. The pointers are represented by vertical and horizontal arrows. As illustrated in Figure 6.6, we can select one of the two rules of laying out these two subpictures. Figure 6.7 shows the visual mapping including these composite rules. A predicate *diagonal* draws a diagonal line in the specified box, which represents a null pointer. To connect a cell to the subpictures by vertical and horizontal arrows, reference points *topleft* and *lefttop* are declared as *top* and *left* of the left box of the cell in a subpicture (see *cell* in Fig. 6.7).[3]

Figure 6.8(a) and 6.8(b) show the resultant pictures of vertical type composition and of horizontal type composition respectively. As these pictures show, the pictures of the former type tend to become vertically long,

---

[3] COOL has the clipping ON/OFF switch. In the clipping mode (default), lines and arrows inside graphical objects are not drawn. As the visual mapping in this application is performed in the non-clipping mode, the parts of arrows inside the cells are drawn without clipping.

```
v( cons( cons( A,  B ), cons( C, D ) ) ) :-
      P = cons( cons( A,  B ), cons( C, D ) ),
      pstart( P ),
      v( cons( A, B ) ),  v( cons( C, D ) ),  cell( P ),
      vertical( [[P, car], cons( A, B )], [left_align] ),
      horizontal( [[P, cdr], cons( C, D )], [top_align] ),
      % vertical type composition
      y_order( [cons( C, D ), cons( A, B )], 17, [ ] ),
      x_order( [[P, cdr], cons( C, D )], 17, [ ] ),
   (    % horizontal type composition                        )
   (    y_order( [[P, car], cons( A, B )], 17, [ ] ),        )
   (    x_order( [cons( A, B ), cons( C, D )], 17, [ ] ),    )
      arrow( [P, car], cons( A, B ), center, topleft, [ ] ),
      arrow( [P, cdr], cons( C, D ), center, lefttop, [ ] ),
      pend.

v( cons( cons( A,  B ), nil ) ) :-
      P = cons( cons( A,  B ), nil ),
      pstart( P ),
      v( cons( A, B ) ),  cell( P ),  diagonal( [P, cdr] ),
      verticallisting( [[P, car], cons( A, B )], 17, [left_align] ),
      arrow( [P, car], cons( A, B ), center, topleft, [ ] ),
      pend.

v( cons( A, cons( B, C ) ) ) :-
      P = cons( A, cons( B, C ) ),
      pstart( P ),
      v( cons( B, C ) ),  cell( P ),  label( [P, car], A, [bound] ),
      horizontallisting( [[P, cdr], cons( B, C )], 17, [top_align] ),
      arrow( [P, cdr], cons( B, C ), center, lefttop, [ ] ),
      pend.

v( cons( A,  nil ) ) :-
      P = cons( A, nil ),
      pstart( P ),
      cell( P ),  label( [P, car], A, [bound] ),  diagonal( [P, cdr] ),
      pend.

cell( P ) :-
      box( [P, car], 17, 17, [bound] ),  box( [P, cdr], 17, 17, [bound] ),
      horizontallisting( [[P, car], [P, cdr]], 0, [ ] ),
      reference( P, topleft, [P, car], top ),  reference( P, lefttop, [P, car], left ).
```

Figure 6.7:   Visual mapping for list diagrams.

(a) vertical type composition

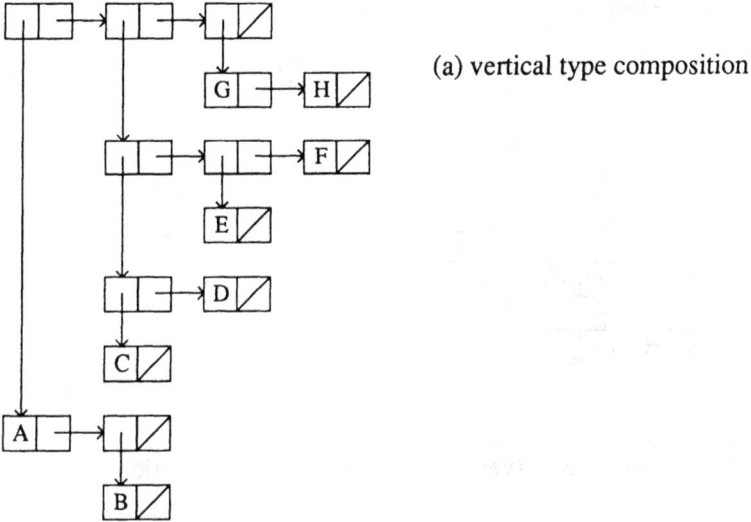

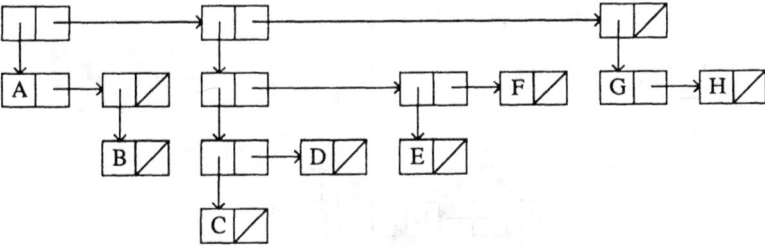

(b) horizontal type composition

Figure 6.8: List diagrams.

Data: ((A (B)) (((C) D) (E) F) (G H))

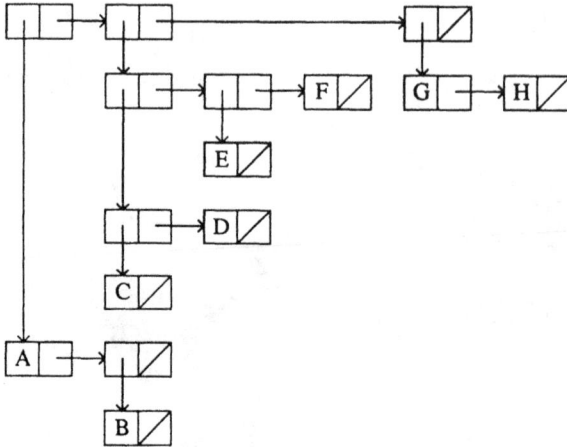

(c) mixed type (vertical and horizontal) composition

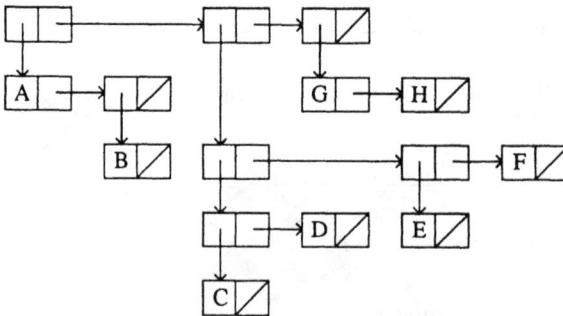

(d) mixed type (horizontal and vertical) composition

Figure 6.8: List diagrams (continued).

and the ones of the latter type tend to become horizontally long. The problem of optimizing the balance of layouts is difficult, as usual. To avoid imbalance of layouts, we try a mixed type composition in which the compositions of these two types are applied by turns. Fig. 6.8(c) and 6.8(d) show the pictures generated by the use of this mixed version. The result shows that this is a simple but good method of avoiding imbalance to some extent. In order to produce more balanced layouts, it might be necessary to choose the appropriate composite rules depending on the given structures.

6.4. Diagrams for Program Structures

We apply TRIP to displaying the structures of programs. The most popular graphical representation of control flows is the flowchart. However, flowcharts do not match high-level structured programming. We use here the structured charts, which are known as Nassi-Shneiderman (NS) diagrams [97], to represent the structures of programs. NS diagrams are used in graphical syntax-directed editors whose users can make programs interactively by editing diagrams [3, 103].

We present a general system by which a source program written in a programming language is translated into the corresponding NS diagram. In this visualization problem, a programming language is the original textual representation and an NS diagram is the target pictorial representation in our words. As the relational structure representation, we use an intermediate universal representation independent of specific languages. This representation is mapped to a diagram based on boxes. Figure 6.9 illustrates the visualization system. The parsers for translating a source program into the intermediate representation are prepared for respective languages.

The visual mapping used for this application is shown in Figure 6.10. We visualize iterative commands and alternative commands as the special boxes. Figure 6.11 shows the NS diagram for a binary search program written in C. The program is translated into the following intermediate representation;

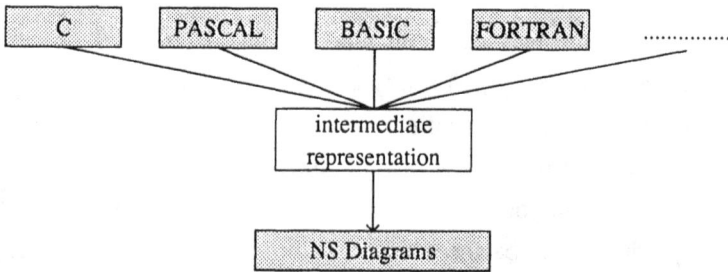

Figure 6.9: A general system for generating NS diagrams.

[header('int binarysearch(int x, int v[], int n)'),
declaration('int low, high, mid;'),
statement('low = 0;'),
statement('high = n - 1;'),
iteration('while (low <= high)' , [
    statement('mid = (low + high) / 2;'),
    alternation('x < v[mid]' ,
      [statement('high = mid - 1;')],
      [alternation('x > v[mid]' ,
        [statement('low = mid + 1;')],
        [statement('return mid;')])])]),
statement('return -1;')]

The visual mapping is applied to this list. Figure 6.12 shows the NS
diagram for a program of Eratosthenes' sieve written in BASIC. Note that a
GOTO-statement is translated into an alternation by the parser. However,
the programs including GOTO-statements can not always be represented by
these diagrams.[4] A larger example is shown in Figure 6.13, which represents

---

[4] Nassi-Shneiderman diagrams were originally developed to support structured
programming, especially GOTO-less programming.

```
%      v( ProgramList, WidthOfDiagram ).
v( [H], WIDTH ) :-
        pstart( [H], [bound] ),
        vline( H, WIDTH ),
        pend.

v( [H l L], WIDTH ) :-
        pstart( [H l L], [bound] ),
        v( L, WIDTH ),
        vline( H, WIDTH ), verticallisting( [H, L], 0, [ ] ),
        pend.

vline( header( S ), WIDTH ) :-
        boxwithlabel( header( S ), WIDTH, 20, S, [left, visible] ).

vline( statement( S ), WIDTH ) :-
        boxwithlabel( statement( S ), WIDTH, 20, S, [left, invisible] ).

vline( declaration( S ), WIDTH ) :-
        boxwithlabel( declaration( S ), WIDTH, 20, S, [left, invisible] ).

vline( iteration( S, BODY ), WIDTH ) :-
        O = iteration( S, BODY ),
        pstart( O, [bound] ),
        NEWWIDTH is WIDTH - 40,
        v( BODY, NEWWIDTH ),
        boxwithlabel( [O, iteration], WIDTH, 20, S, [left, invisible] ),
        verticallisting( [[O, iteration], BODY], 0, [right_align] ),
        pend.

vline( alternation( S, TRUE, FALSE ), WIDTH ) :-
        O = alternation( S, TRUE, FALSE ),
        pstart( O, [bound] ),
        NEWWIDTH is WIDTH / 2,
        v( TRUE, NEWWIDTH ), v( FALSE, NEWWIDTH ),
        boxwithlabel( [O, alternation], WIDTH, 20, S, [top, bound] ),
        separateline( [O, alternation] ),
        label( [O, alternation], 'T', [left] ), label( [O, alternation], 'F', [right] ),
        verticallisting( [[O, alternation], TRUE], 0, [left_align] ),
        verticallisting( [[O, alternation], FALSE], 0, [right_align] ),
        pend.

% vline( alternation( S, [ ], FALSE ), WIDTH ) and vline( alternation( S, TRUE, [ ] ),
% WIDTH ) are defined in the same way.
```

Figure 6.10:   Visual mapping for NS diagrams.

INPUT DATA:

```
int binarysearch(int x, int v[], int n)
{
int low, high, mid;
low = 0;
high = n - 1;
while (low <= high) {
mid = (low + high) / 2;
if (x < v[mid])
high = mid - 1;
else if(x > v[mid])
low = mid + 1;
else
return mid;
}
return -1;
}
```

int binarysearch(int x, int v[], int n)			
int low, high, mid;			
low = 0;			
high = n - 1;			
while (low <= high)			
	mid = (low + high) / 2;		
	T x < v[mid] F		
	high = mid - 1;	T x > v[mid] F	
		low = mid + 1;	return mid;
return -1;			

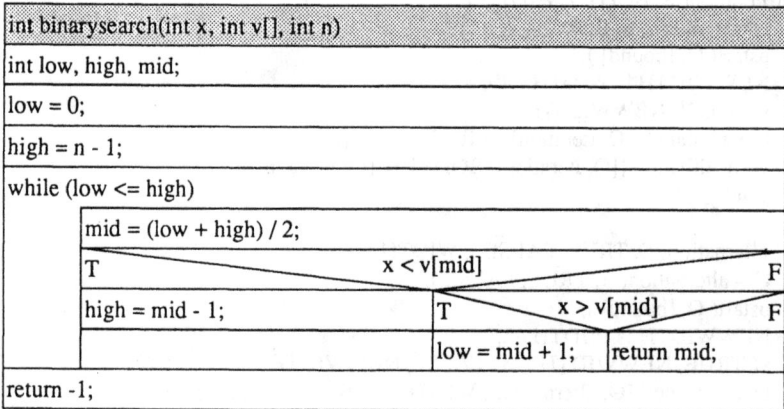

Figure 6.11: An NS diagram for binary search program (C).

INPUT DATA:

```
10 'Prime Numbers (Eratosthenes)
20 DIM P(100)
30 MAX = 100
40 FOR I = 2 TO MAX
50 P(I) = 1
60 NEXT I
70 FOR I = 2 TO MAX
80 IF P(I) = 0 GOTO 130
90 PRINT I
100 FOR J = I TO MAX STEP I
110 P(J) = 0
120 NEXT J
130 NEXT I
```

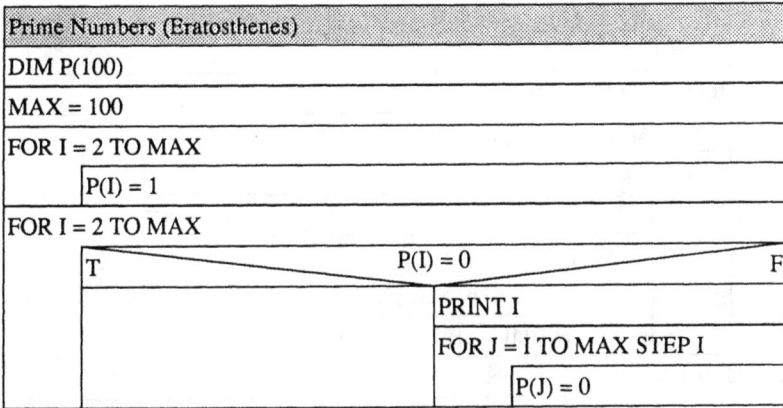

Figure 6.12: An NS diagram for Eratosthenes' sieve (BASIC).

procedure gauss;

```
i, j, p, m : integer;
s : real;
t : arrary[1..n] of integer;
for i := 1 to n do
    t[i] := i;
for p := 1 to n do
    m := p;
    for i := p+1 to n do
        T ╱      abs(a[t[i],p])>abs(a[t[m],p])      ╲ F
        m := i;
    i := t[m];
    t[m] := t[p];
    t[p] := i;
    for j := p+1 to n+1 do
        a[t[p],j] := a[t[p],j] / a[t[p],p];
    for i := 1 to n do
        T ╱               i <> p               ╲ F
        for j := p+1 to n+1 do
            s := a[t[i],p] * a[t[p],j];
            a[t[i],j] := a[t[i],j] - s
for i := 1 to n do
    ans[i] := a[t[i],n+1]
```

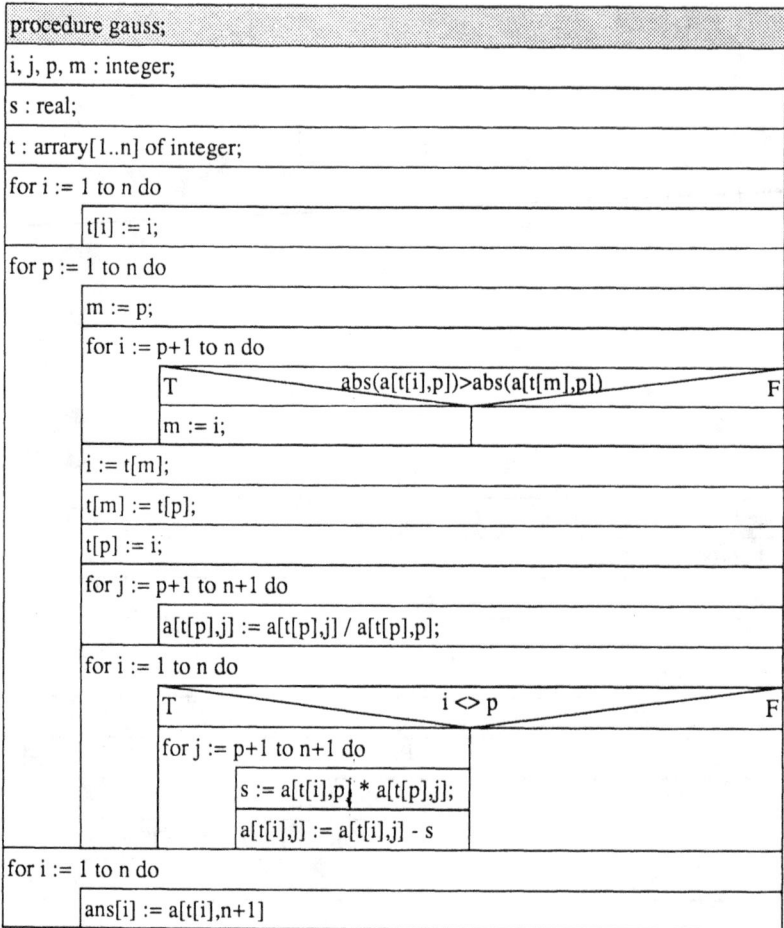

Figure 6.13:   An NS diagram for Gaussian elimination (PASCAL).

Gaussian elimination written in PASCAL. (The source program is omitted in Fig. 6.13.)

We can extend this system to a more elaborate version by introducing the special handling of variable declarations, SWITCH-statements, and procedure calls.

6.5. Entity-Relationship Diagrams

The entity-relationship (ER) model has been widely used to represent the schema of a database. Entity-relationship diagrams are very useful to visualize the structure of data based on this model [31, 135]. Some algorithms for automatic layout of ER diagrams are studied (for example, [128]). Recently database systems with the visual interface, whose users can manipulate databases by editing their graph representations directly, are developed [25, 77]. We present a system for drawing ER diagrams from the non-graphical ER schema description as an application of TRIP. The layout of ER diagrams is computed by the use of our graph drawing algorithm.

We describe an ER schema in Prolog. We can use another textual language for describing an ER schema, if we prepare the translator from the language into the Prolog representation. A predicate *entity* defines an entity set and its attributes. A predicate *relationship* defines a relationship between entity sets. We assume that relationships are binary. Here we visualize an ER schema for an educational institute, which is described as follows;

> *% entity(ENTITY, ATTRIBUTES).*
> *entity(institute, [name]).*
> *entity(course, [code, name]).*
> *entity(student, [number, name, grade]).*
> *% relationship(RELATION, ENTITY1, ENTITY2, #1, #2).*
> *relationship('C-I', course, institute, n, 1).*
> *relationship('S-I', student, institute, n, 1).*
> *relationship('S-C', student, course, m, n).*

The forth and fifth arguments of *relationship* represent the cardinality of a relationship. For example, the C-I relationship is of cardinality $n : 1$.

According to the convention of drawing ER diagrams, we represent entity sets, attributes, and relationships as boxes, ellipses, and diamonds respectively. As for line connections, we adopt straight line connections between a box and an ellipse, and between a box and a diamond. Figure 6.14 shows the visual mapping for ER diagrams. The positions of boxes and ellipses are computed by the graph layout system. A diamond is placed between the boxes which the diamond is connected to. The cardinality of a relationship is visualized as the labels associated with the connecting lines. Figure 6.15(a) illustrates the resultant picture. The layout is balanced pleasingly. However, one may find that some connecting lines are too short. It is because the graph layout system regards the distance between objects as the distance between the centers of them. It could be solved by using the distance between the nearest points in the objects instead of the distance between the centers in the graph layout system.

Next, we add the following data to the above ER schema;

      entity(teacher, [name, salary]).

      relationship('I-T', institute, teacher, 1, n).

      relationship('C-T', course, teacher, m, n).

The ER diagram for the updated data is shown in Fig. 6.15(b). We can build a visual database browser by combining this visualization technique with a direct manipulation interface. In the same way, we can apply TRIP to the generation of state diagrams and data flow diagrams as well as ER diagrams.

```
%      mapping for entity predicates
entitymap :-
      entity( ENTITY, ATTRIBUTES ),
      boxwithlabel( ENTITY, 50, 20, ENTITY, [bound] ),
      attributemap( ENTITY, ATTRIBUTES ),
      fail.

attributemap( _, [ ] ).
attributemap( ENTITY, [H | L] ) :-
      ellipsewithlabel( [ENTITY | H], 20, 10, H, [bound] ),
      adjacent( ENTITY, [ENTITY | H], 1 ),       % entry to graph layout system
      connect( ENTITY, [ENTITY | H], center, center, [straight] ),
      attributemap( ENTITY, L ).

%      mapping for relationship predicates
relationshipmap :-
      relationship( R, ENTITY1, ENTITY2, M, N ),
      diamondwithlabel( [R], 50, 30, R, [visible] ),
      adjacent( ENTITY1, ENTITY2, 3 ),           % entry to graph layout system
      between( [R], ENTITY1, ENTITY2, [ ] ),
      connectwithlabel( ENTITY1, [R], center, center, [straight], M ),
      connectwithlabel( ENTITY2, [R], center, center, [straight], N ),
      fail.
```

Figure 6.14: Visual mapping for ER diagrams.

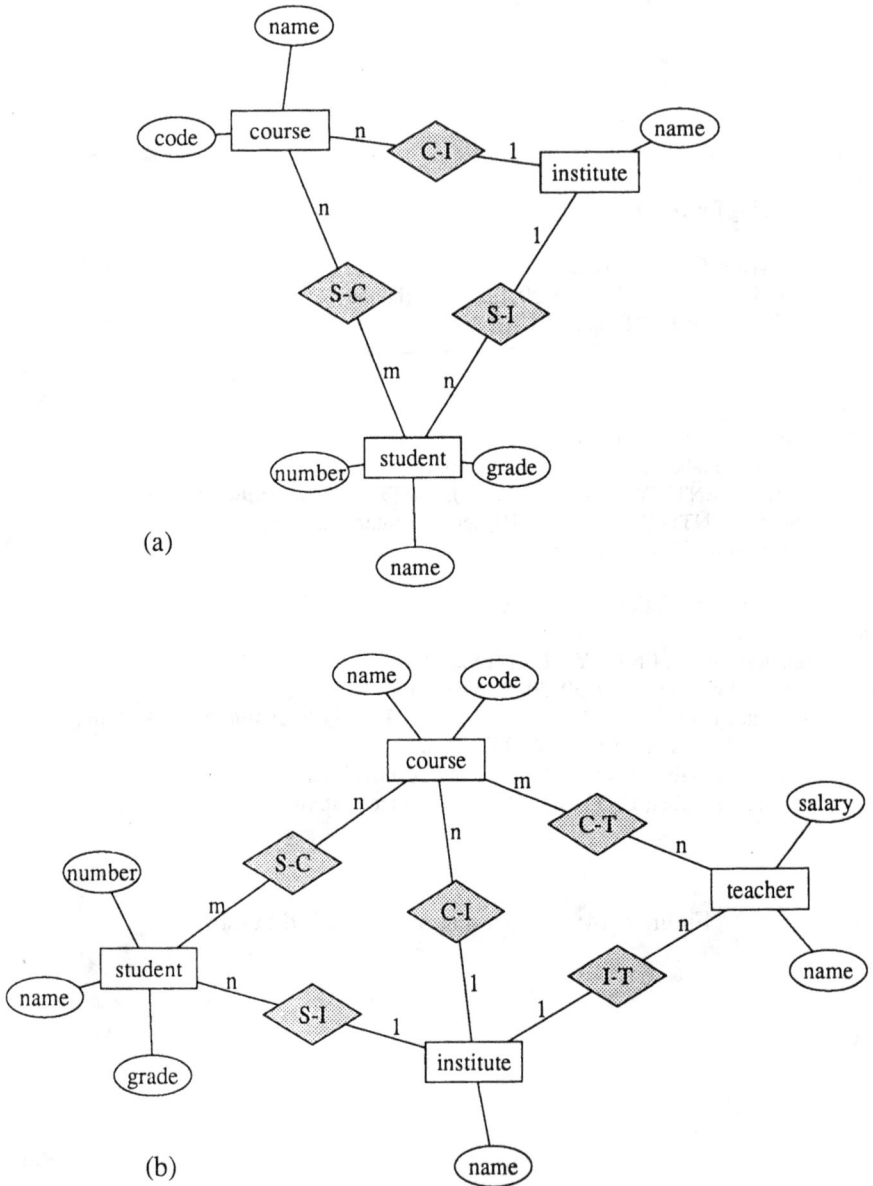

Figure 6.15: Entity-relationship diagrams.

CHAPTER 7

INVERSE TRANSLATION

So far we have focused on the visualization of information, that is, the translation from textual or internal representations into pictorial representations. In this chapter, we describe the translation from pictorial representations into textual or internal representations, which is also an important part of visual communication between human and computer. The presented visualization framework is so general that it can be applied to this inverse translation. First we take up an application to direct manipulation systems, and next we propose a general image recognition framework.

7.1. Toward Intelligent Direct Manipulation Systems

Direct manipulation[1] is commonly admitted to be a good principle of the interactive user interface [59, 60, 116, 117, 143]. Macintosh computer

---

[1] Though the concept of direct manipulation has not been defined precisely, it is usually interpreted as the feeling that users are involved directly with the computer's activities.

has realized this principle successfully [5]. We apply our visualization framework to direct manipulation systems, and propose a direction toward the intelligent user interface.

In a direct manipulation system, internal data is represented as a pictorial form and is manipulated by physical actions on the pictorial form. We consider a general graphical editor by which relational data is edited through a pre-defined pictorial form. The data to be edited is assumed to be described based on the relational structure representation in our model. The pictorial form is specified by the user-defined visual mapping. Accordingly users can change the pictorial form freely by changing the visual mapping. For simplicity, the system supports only creation and deletion of a single data item as the editing commands. The interaction in this system consists of three successive phases, as follows.

(1) Users create a graphical object at an appropriate position, or delete a graphical object by picking it up.

(2) The system updates the visual structure according to the users' actions, and propagates the modification to the relational structure.

(3) The system updates the pictorial representation, i.e., redraws the picture, according to the modification of the internal data.

Figure 7.1 illustrates this interaction model. We do not discuss here the details of the user interface such as how to create or delete a graphical object by operating with a pointing device.

When users want to add a new item to the members of a relation, the specifying manner would be tedious if they must exactly specify which relation to be modified and where to insert the new member. In this case, can the system insert a new item into an appropriate position of an appropriate relation automatically from the created position of the new object? Such an enhanced semantic feedback is one of the requirements of advanced directed manipulation systems. We try to solve this problem. Consider the following simple example. In this example, relations *relation_A(a, [b, c, d, e])*

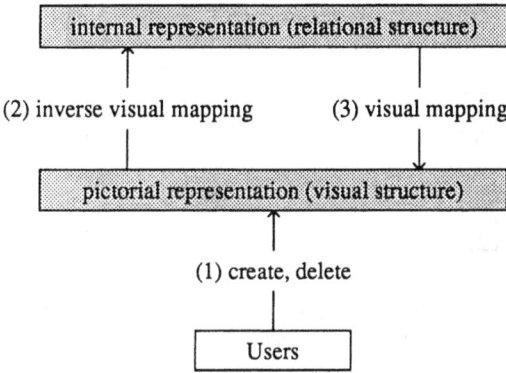

Figure 7.1:   The interaction model of proposed graphical editor.

and *relation_B(p, [q, r, s])* are edited. They are visualized as a circular layout and a tree layout respectively as follows;

> *relation_A(a, [b, c, d, e]) ->*
> *circularlisting(a, [b, c, d, e], [ ]),*
> *verticallisting([b, a], 40, [ ]),*
> *multi_connect([a], [b, c, d, e], center, center, [straight]).*
> *relation_B(p, [q, r, s]) ->*
> *above([p], [q, r, s], 60, [ ]),*
> *horizontallisting([q, r, s], 40, [ ]),*
> *multi_connect([p], [q, r, s], bottom, top, [orthogonal]).*

Now we want to create a new graphical object *x* and add it to the members of either relation. Figure 7.2(a) shows the pictorial representation in the initial state. When *x* is created at the position (1), it should be inserted into *relation_A* as illustrated in Fig. 7.2(b). In the same way, when *x* is created at the position (2), it should be inserted into *relation_B* as illustrated in Fig. 7.2(c).

First of all, we discuss this problem as a geometric problem. If *x* is inserted into *relation_A* , the relation will result in one of the four cases;

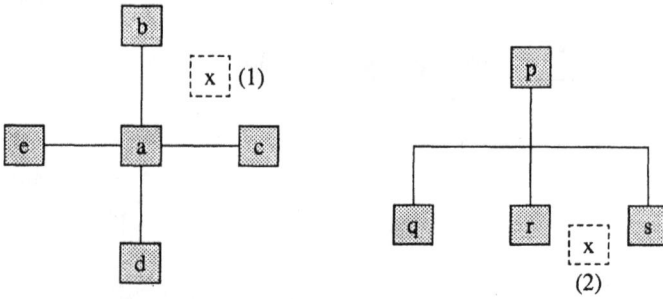

(a) initial pictorial representation
relation_A(a, [b, c, d, e]), relation_B(p, [q, r, s]).

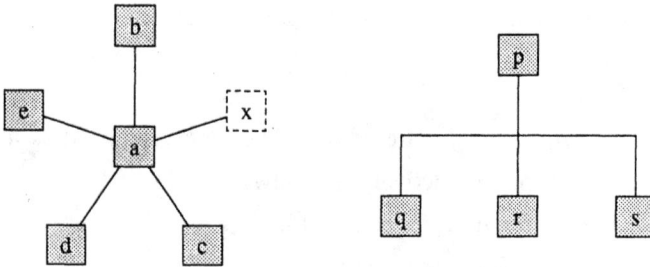

(b) create a new object **x** at the position (1)
relation_A(a, [b, x, c, d, e]), relation_B(p, [q, r, s]).

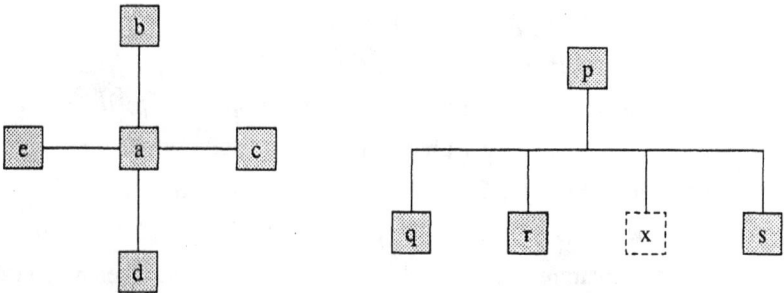

(c) create a new object **x** at the position (2)
relation_A(a, [b, c, d, e]), relation_B(p, [q, r, x, s]).

Figure 7.2:   An intelligent interface for modifying relations.

$\qquad$ *relation_A(a, [b, x, c, d, e]),*

$\qquad$ *relation_A(a, [b, c, x, d, e]),*

$\qquad$ *relation_A(a, [b, c, d, x, e]),*

$\qquad$ *relation_A(a, [b, c, d, e, x]).*

These cases generate different new layouts, one of which Fig. 7.2(b) shows. Likewise there are four candidates for a new layout if x is inserted into *relation_B*. Here we represent a layout as P which is a vector of all variables in the layout. Let $P_1, P_2, ..., P_n$ be these layout candidates, and P be the current layout including a new object. Then, the most appropriate layout can be defined as the nearest layout to P. The Euclidean distance can be used as the distance between P and P_i. That is, the problem results in finding P_i that satisfies

$$dis\,(P - P_i) = \min_{1 \le j \le n} dis\,(P - P_j).$$

Though this geometric problem can be solved by an exhaustive computation, it seems too slow to the interactive interface. We propose an approximate method of finding an appropriate layout from the geometric data. First we prepare bounding boxes for respective relations. When a new object is created, a relation is examined if and only if its bounding box encloses the object. Next we test whether each insertion position is appropriate or not for a candidate relation. To realize this test, we introduce the testing functions which evaluate constraints and estimate errors. The testing functions return *true* if the errors are within a certain range, and return *false* otherwise. For example, in the case of the above *relation_A*, the following tests are executed in the order;

$\qquad$ *circular_cond(a, [b, x, c, d, e]),*

$\qquad$ *circular_cond(a, [b, c, x, d, e]),*

$\qquad$ *circular_cond(a, [b, c, d, x, e]),*

$\qquad$ *circular_cond(a, [b, c, d, e, x]),*

where *circular_cond* is the testing function for a *circularlisting* relation. Similar tests are generated for each relation. We can realize the enhanced

semantic feedback described above by integrating this inference mechanism
into the system.

We can build an intelligent direct manipulation system by using this
approach. The basis of our interaction model is the distinct separation of
visual structures from relational structures. Users manipulate only visual
structures, and the consistency between visual structures and relational
structures is maintained by the translation mappings between them. Such a
general framework is important for the systematic generation of interactive
user interface modules.

7.2. A General Image Recognition Framework

A number of image recognition systems are developed for different purposes. However, many of them are implemented in ad hoc and domain-
dependent manners. A general image recognition framework is necessary
for developing a system which can handle a wide range of image recognition
problems. In this section, we apply our visualization framework to the generalization of image recognition problems.

Image recognition is the translation from pictorial representations into
textual or internal representations. This translation process can be regarded
as the inverse translation of the visualization we have discuss so far. Figure
7.3 illustrates this process, whose flow is the inverse of the one in Fig. 3.2.
In the first stage of this inverse translation, graphical objects are recognized
from an input image, and graphical relations (including geometric relations)
among the objects are detected. To realize this, we require an efficient spatial parsing technique [76]. The inverse visual mapping is considered as the
literal inverse mapping of the visual mapping. Graphical objects are
mapped to abstract objects, and graphical relations among them are mapped
to abstract relations among the corresponding abstract objects. A syn-
thesizer generates a target textual or internal representation.

In a tool based on this framework, users could get their desired image
recognition systems by specifying the inverse visual mapping data. In

target textual representation

```
        ↑
┌───────────────────┐
│    Synthesizer    │<--------  syntax data
└───────────────────┘
        ↑
```

relational structure representation

```
       ↑
┌────────────────────┐
│Inverse Visual Mapping│<--------  mapping data
└────────────────────┘
       ↑
```

visual structure representation

```
       ↑
┌───────────────────┐
│   Spatial Parser   │<--------  parsing data
└───────────────────┘
       ↑
```

original pictorial representation

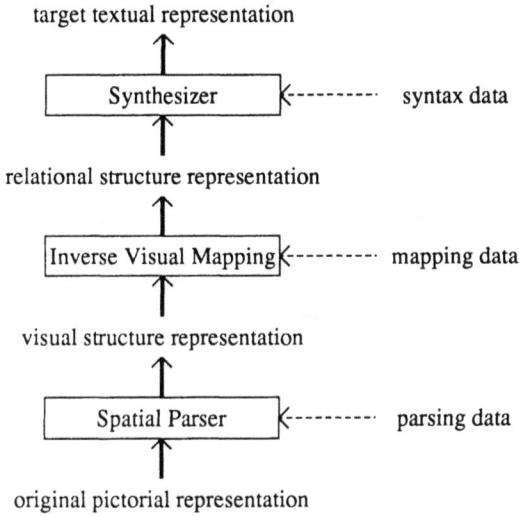

Figure 7.3:   Proposed image recognition model.

addition, we can extend this model to the automatic beautifier for drawings like [99]. Such a system finds and infers geometric constraints among graphical objects from a rough drawing, and generates a pleasing drawing which satisfies the constraints. We can use COOL to solve constraints and generate a picture in this system.

CHAPTER 8

CONCLUDING REMARKS

The visualization of information involves many issues other than the problems described in this book. Our research has concentrated on the visualization of abstract objects and relations. We are going to extend our visualization framework and introduce new ideas in order to handle a wider range of visualization problems.

We have some future extensions in the visual mapping, the COOL system, and the graph drawing algorithm, as described in Chapter 3, 4, and 5 respectively. In Chapter 7, we have proposed the inverse visual mapping and its applications. In addition to these work, the following topics should be studied in the future.

Application to Animation

Our system can be applied to the translation from textual representations into animations by introducing temporal relations or temporal visual mapping. To realize this, COOL must be extended so that it can handle time dependency of constraints, like Animus [38] which is an animation system using temporal constraints. In addition, powerful constraint solving technique is necessary for handling dynamic constraints.

Integration of Knowledge-Based Systems

In Chapter 6, we have presented the applications for the visualization of knowledge described in a natural language. Relational structures in our visualization framework can be represented and manipulated efficiently in knowledge-based systems. A variety of visual mapping data can be also maintained flexibly in these systems. Constructing an intelligent visualization system on a large knowledge-based system is a promising research topic in the next generation.

Study on Cognitive Aspects of Visualization

The problem of how to choose an appropriate and effective pictorial representation is greatly relevant to our research. We can say only vaguely which representations are easy to understand for given information. To solve this problem clearly, we must study the mechanism of human cognition. The researchers in cognitive science and human factors are studying this problem intensively. We are going to note and use the results in this area in order to build a visualization database and automate the visual mapping.

Bidirectional Translation among Textual and Visual Languages

As we have described in Chapter 7, we can take the same approach toward the translation from visual languages into textual languages. It might be possible to translate a pictorial representation into another pictorial representation through an intermediate representation in our model. We need textual representations in some cases and pictorial representations in other cases even for the same data. The long-term goal of our research is to construct an integrated system in which textual world and visual world are connected to each other by bidirectional translation.

Finally, we believe that our research greatly contributes to the visualization of various kinds of information handled in information systems. We are going to continue this work and are expecting that many researchers will have interests in our research and the visualization.

APPENDIX

We list up the whole visual mapping of the application in Section 6.1. By the visual mapping, specific patterns of case relations are mapped to the corresponding graphical objects and graphical relations. We also present the definition of *family* relation in Section 6.2.

(1) The visual mapping in Section 6.1.

```
objectmap :- o1; o2.
relationmap :- r1; r2; r3; r4; r5; r6; r7; r8; r9; r10.

%            [ plural objects ]
o1 :- semantics( [be, _, ag(and( AL )), comp( C )] ),
      objects( AL, C ),
      fail.
%            [ singular object ]
o2 :- semantics( [be, _, ag( A ), comp( C )] ),
      object( A, C ),
      fail.
%            [ place, put, lay (vt), and lie (vi) ]
r1 :- semantics( [place, _, ag( _ ), obj( O ), loc( L )] ),
      locate( O, L ),
      fail.
```

```
r2 :-   semantics( [put, _, ag( _ ), obj( O ), loc( L )] ),
        locate( O, L ),
        fail.
r3 :-   semantics( [lay, _, ag( _ ), obj( O ), loc( L )] ),
        locate( O, L ),
        fail.
r4 :-   semantics( [lie, _, ag( A ), loc( L )] ),
        locate( A, L ),
        fail.
%              [ arrange horizontally or vertically ]
r5 :-   semantics( [arrange, _, ag( _ ), obj( O ), loc( L )] ),
        arrange( O, L ),
        fail.
%              [ put ... with a connecting line ]
r6 :-   semantics( [put, _, ag( _ ), obj( O ), loc( L ), part(with( V ))] ),
        locate_conn( O, L, V ),
        fail.
%              [ connect to ]
r7 :-   semantics( [connect, _, ag( A ), obj( O ), goal(to( G ))] ),
        conn_and( A, O, G ),
        fail.
r8 :-   semantics( [connect, _, ag( A ), obj(and( [X, Y] ))] ),
        conn_and( A, X, Y ),
        fail.
%              [ hide and contain ]
r9 :-   semantics( [hide, _, ag( A ), obj( O )] ),
        hide_and( A, O ),
        fail.
r10 :-  semantics( [contain, _, ag( A ), obj( O )] ),
        contain_and( A, O ),
        fail.


objects( [ ], _ ).
objects( [A | L], C ) :-
        object( A, C ), objects( L, C ).
object( [X | _], [box | PROP] ) :-
        getobjprop( PROP, L, W, H, R ),
        boxwithlabel( X, W, H, X, L ).
object( [X | _], [diamond | PROP] ) :-
        getobjprop( PROP, L, W, H, R ),
        diamondwithlabel( X, W, H, X, L ).
object( [X | _], [circle | PROP] ) :-
        getobjprop( PROP, L, W, H, R ),
        circlewithlabel( X, R, X, L ).


%              [ prepositions ]
%              on the left (right) of, above, below, on, under, between
```

locate([X | _], on([left, def-arti, relation(of([Y | _])), singular])) :-
        horizontallisting([X, Y], 30, [ ]), !.
locate(X, on([right, def-arti, relation(of(Y)), singular])) :-
        locate(Y, on([left, def-arti, relation(of(X)), singular])), !.
locate(XL, above(YL)) :-
        getlist(XL, XO), getlist(YL, YO), above(XO, YO, 30, [ ]).
locate([X | _], on([Y | _])) :-
        verticallisting([X, Y], 0, [ ]).
locate(X, below(Y)) :- locate(Y, above(X)).
locate(X, under(Y)) :- locate(Y, on(X)).
locate([X | _], between(and([[Y | _], [Z | _]]))) :- between(X, Y, Z, [ ]).

locate_conn(X, on([right, def-arti, relation(of(Y)), singular]), V) :-
        locate(X, on([right, def-arti, relation(of(Y)), singular])),
        conn_and(V, X, Y).
locate_conn(X, on([left, def-arti, relation(of(Y)), singular]), V) :-
        locate_conn(Y, on([right, def-arti, relation(of(X)), singular]), V).
locate_conn(X, above(Y), V) :-
        locate(X, above(Y)),
        conn_and(V, X, Y).
locate_conn(X, below(Y), V) :- locate_conn(Y, above(X), V).

arrange(OL, horizontally) :-
        getlist(OL, X),
        horizontallisting(X, 30, [ ]).
arrange(OL, vertically) :-
        getlist(OL, X),
        verticallisting(X, 30, [ ]).

conn_and([line | PROP], OL, GL) :-
        getlist(OL, X), getlist(GL, Y),
        getlineprop(PROP, P),
        multi_connect(X, Y, center, center, P).

hide_and(AL, OL) :-
        getlist(AL, X), getlist(OL, Y),
        multi_hide(X, Y).

contain_and([X | _], [Y | _]) :- contain(X, Y, 0, [center_align]).
contain_and([X | _], and([[Y | _], [Z | _]])) :-
        contain(X, Y, 10, [left_align]),
        contain(X, Z, 10, [right_align]).

%   [adjectives]
getlineprop(L, P) :-
        getprop(L, PL), !,
        mkprop(PL, P).

```
mkprop( [ ], [ ] ).
mkprop( [[X, _] | L], [X | P] ) :- mkprop( L, P ).

getobjprop( L, P, W, H, R ) :-
        getprop( L, PL ), !,
        getobjsize( PL, W, H, R ),
        getobjcol( PL, P ).
getobjsize( PL, W, H, R ) :-
        member( [large, [very]], PL ) ->      W = 150, H = 75, R = 75;
        member( [large, [ ]], PL ) ->         W = 80, H = 40, R = 40;
        member( [standard, [ ]], PL ) ->      W = 60, H = 30, R = 30;
        member( [small, [ ]], PL ) ->         W = 40, H = 20, R = 20;
        member( [small, [very]], PL ) ->      W = 30, H = 15, R = 15;
                                              W = 60, H = 30, R = 30.
getobjcol( PL, P ) :-
        member( [white, [ ]], PL ) ->   P = [bound];
        member( [black, [ ]], PL ) ->   P = [visible];
                                        P = [ ].

getprop( [ ], [ ] ).
getprop( [properties( L ) | _], L ).
getprop( [_ | L], P ) :- getprop( L, P ).

getlist( [X | _], [ X ] ).
getlist( and( L ), O ) :- getandlist( L, O ).
getandlist( [ ], [ ] ).
getandlist( [[X | _] | L], [X | O] ) :- getandlist( L, O ).
```

(2) The family relation in Section 6.2.

```prolog
wife_of( W, H ) :-
      semantics( [be, _, ag( [W | _] ),
      comp( [wife, def-arti, relation(of( [H | _] )), singular] )] ).
husband_of( H, W ) :-
      semantics( [be, _, ag( [H | _]·),
      comp( [husband, def-arti, relation(of( [W | _] )), singular] )] ).
mother_of( M, [C] ) :-
      semantics( [be, _, ag( [M | _] ),
      comp( [mother, def-arti, relation(of( [C | _] )), singular] )] ).
father_of( F, [C] ) :-
      semantics( [be, _, ag( [F | _] ),
      comp( [father, def-arti, relation(of( [C | _] )), singular] )] ).
children_of( [C], P ) :-
      semantics( [be, _, ag( [C | _] ),
      comp( [child, def-arti, relation(of( [P | _] )), singular] )] ).
children_of( C, P ) :-
      semantics( [be, _, ag(and( L )),
      comp( [child, def-arti, relation(of( [P | _] )), plural] )] ),
      getlist( L, C ).


family( F, M, C ) :-
      parents( F, M ), children( C, F ), persons( [F, M | C] ).
family( F, M, C ) :-
      parents( F, M ), children( C, M ), persons( [F, M | C] ).
family( F, M, C ) :-
      father_of( F, C ), children_of( C, M ), persons( [F, M | C] ).
family( F, M, C ) :-
      mother_of( M, C ), children_of( C, F ), persons( [F, M | C] ).
family( F, M, C ) :-
      mother_of( M, C ), father_of( F, C ), persons( [F, M | C] ).
parents( F, M ) :-
      wife_of( M, F ); husband_of( F, M ).
children( C, P ) :-
      children_of( C, P ); mother_of( P, C ); father_of( P, C ).


person( [ ] ).
persons( [ ] ).
persons( [H | L] ) :-
      person( H ) -> persons( L );
      person( [ ] ) -> retract(person( [ ] )),
            asserta(person( H )), persons( L );
            asserta(person( H )), persons( L ).


getlist([], []).
getlist([[X|_]|L], [X|O]) :- getlist(L, O).
```

REFERENCES

1. Adobe Systems Inc., *PostScript Language Reference Manual,* Addison-Wesley, 1986.

2. A. V. Aho, R. Sethi, and J. D. Ullman, *Compilers - Principles, Techniques, and Tools,* Addison-Wesley, 1986.

3. M. B. Albizuri-Romero, "GRASE - A Graphical Syntax-Directed Editor for Structured Programming," *ACM SIGPLAN Notices,* vol. 19, no. 2, pp. 28-37, Feb. 1984.

4. ANSI, "American National Standard for the functional specification of the programmer's hierarchical interactive graphics standard (PHIGS)," ANSI/X3H3, American National Standards Institute, New York, 1983.

5. Apple Computer Inc., *Human Interface Guidelines: The Apple Desktop Interface,* Addison-Wesley, 1987.

6. Y. Arens, L. Miller, S. C. Shapiro, and N. K. Sondheimer, "Automatic Construction of User-Interface Displays," *Proc. of AAAI-88,* pp. 808-813, Minnesota, Aug. 1988.

7. P. S. Barth, "An Object-Oriented Approach to Graphical Interfaces," *ACM Trans. Graphics,* vol. 5, no. 2, pp. 142-172, Apr. 1986.

8. C. Batini, E. Nardelli, and R. Tamassia, "A Layout Algorithm for Data Flow Diagrams," *IEEE Trans. Software Eng.,* vol. SE-12, no. 4, pp. 538-546, Apr. 1986.

9. G. Battista and R. Tamassia, "Algorithms for Plane Representations of Acyclic Digraphs," *Theoretical Computer Science,* vol. 61, no. 2, 3, pp. 175-198, Nov. 1988.

10. B. Becker and G. Hotz, "On the Optimal Layout of Planar Graphs with Fixed Boundary," *SIAM J. Comput.,* vol. 16, no. 5, pp. 946-972, Oct. 1987.

11. M. Behzad, G. Chartrand, and L. Lesniak-Foster, *Graphs & Digraphs,* Prindle, Weber & Schmidt, Boston, 1979.

12. J. L. Bentley, L. W. Jelinski, and B. W. Kernighan, "CHEM - A Program for Typesetting Chemical Diagrams: User Manual," Technical Rep. No. 122, AT&T Bell Lab., Apr. 1986.

13. J. L. Bentley and B. W. Kernighan, "GRAP - A Language for Typesetting Graphs," *Comm. ACM*, vol. 29, no. 8, pp. 782-792, Aug. 1986.

14. J. L. Bentley and B. W. Kernighan, "A System for Algorithm Animation: Tutorial and User Manual," Technical Rep. No. 132, AT&T Bell Lab., Jan. 1987.

15. M. A. Bernard, "On the Automated Drawing of Graphs," *Proc. of 3rd Caribbean Conf. on Combinatorics and Computing*, pp. 43-55, 1981.

16. D. G. Bobrow, L. G. DeMichiel, R. P. Gabriel, S. E. Keene, G. Kiczales, and D. A. Moon, "Common Lisp Object System Specification," *ACM SIGPLAN Notices*, vol. 23, Sep. 1988.

17. A. Borning, "The Programming Language Aspects of ThingLab, A Constraint-Oriented Simulation Laboratory," *ACM Trans. Prog. Lang. and Systems*, vol. 3, no. 4, pp. 353-387, Oct. 1981.

18. A. Borning, "Graphically Defining New Building Blocks in ThingLab," *Human-Computer Interaction*, vol. 2, pp. 269-295, 1986.

19. A. Borning and R. Duisberg, "Constraint-Based Tools for Building User Interfaces," *ACM Trans. Graphics*, vol. 5, no. 4, pp. 345-374, Oct. 1986.

20. A. Borning, R. Duisberg, and B. Freeman-Benson, "Constraint Hierarchies," *Proc. of OOPSLA '87*, pp. 48-60, Oct. 1987.

21. A. D. Brown, "Automated Placement and Routing," *Computer-Aided Design*, vol. 20, no. 1, pp. 39-44, Jan./Feb. 1988.

22. M. H. Brown, *Algorithm Animation,* MIT Press, 1988.

23. M. H. Brown and R. Sedgewick, "A System for Algorithm Animation," *Computer Graphics*, vol. 18, no. 3, pp. 177-186, Jul. 1984.

24. B. Buchberger, "Gröbner bases: An Algorithmic Method in Polynomial Ideal Theory," Technical Rep., CAMP-LINZ, 1983.

25. L. M. Burns, J. L. Archibald, and A. Malhotra, "A Graphical Entity-Relationship Database Browser," Research Rep. RC 13238, IBM Watson Research Center, New York, 1987.

26. P. M. Caporal and G. J. Hahn, "Tools for Automated Statistical Graphics," *IEEE Computer Graphics and Applications*, vol. 1, no. 4, pp. 72-82, Oct. 1981.

27. M. Carpano, "Automatic Display of Hierarchized Graphs for Computer-aided Decision Analysis," *IEEE Trans. Syst., Man, Cybern.*, vol. SMC-10, no. 11, pp. 705-715, Nov. 1980.

28. S. K. Chang, "Visual Languages: A Tutorial and Survey," *IEEE Software*, vol. 4, no. 1, pp. 29-39, Jan. 1987.

29. S. K. Chang, *Principles of Pictorial Information Systems Design,* Prentice-Hall, Englewood Cliffs, 1989.

30. N. Chapin, "New Format for Flowcharts," *Software-Practice and Experience*, vol. 4, no. 4, pp. 341-357, Apr. 1974.

31. P. P. Chen, "The Entity Relationship Model - Towards a unified view of data," *ACM Trans. Database Systems*, vol. 1, no. 1, pp. 9-36, Mar. 1976.

32. N. Chiba, K. Onoguchi, and T. Nishizeki, "Drawing Plane Graphs Nicely," *Acta Informatica*, vol. 22, no. 2, pp. 187-201, Jul. 1985.

33. A. Colmerauer, "Opening the Prolog III Universe," *BYTE*, vol. 12, no. 8, pp. 177-182, Aug. 1987.

34. D. G. Corneil and C. C. Gotlieb, "An Efficient Algorithm for Graph Isomorphism," *J. ACM*, vol. 17, no. 1, pp. 51-64, Jan. 1970.

35. S. K. Debray, *The SB-Prolog System, Version 2.2: A User Manual*, Dept. of Computer Science, Univ. of Arizona, 1987.

36. E. Derman and C. J. Van Wyk, "A Simple Equation Solver and its Application to Financial Modelling," *Software-Practice and Experience*, vol. 14, no. 12, pp. 1169-1181, Dec. 1984.

37. M. S. Dionne and A. K. Mackworth, "ANTICS: A System for Animating LISP Programs," *Computer Graphics and Image Processing*, vol. 7, no. 1, pp. 105-119, Feb. 1978.

38. R. A. Duisberg, "Animation Using Temporal Constraints: An Overview of the Animus System," *Human-Computer Interaction*, vol. 3, pp. 275-307, 1987/1988.

39. P. Eades, "A Heuristics for Graph Drawing," *Congressus Numerantium*, vol. 42, pp. 149-160, May 1984.

40. P. Eades. "Symmetry Finding Algorithms," *Computational Morphology*, 1988.

41. P. Eades and D. Kelly, "Heuristics for Drawing 2-Layered Networks," *Ars Combinatoria 21A*, pp. 89-98, May 1986.

42. P. Eades, B. McKay, and N. Wormald, "On an Edge Crossing Problem," *Proc. of 9th Australian Computer Science Conf.*, pp. 327-334, 1986.

43. P. Eades and H. C. Ng, "An Algorithm for Detecting Symmetries in Drawings," *Ars Combinatoria 23A*, pp. 95-104, 1987.

44. P. Eades and R. Tamassia, "Algorithms for Drawing Graphs: An Annotated Bibliography," Technical Rep. No. CS-89-09, Dept. of Computer Science, Brown Univ., Rhode Island, Feb. 1989.

45. G. Enderle, K. Kansy, and G. Pfaff, *Computer Graphics Programming GKS - The Graphics Standard*, Springer-Verlag, Berlin, 1984.

46. O. Ferstl, "Flowcharting by Stepwise Refinement," *ACM SIGPLAN Notices*, vol. 13, no. 1, pp. 34-42, Jan. 1978.

47. R. W. Floyd, "Algorithm 97: Shortest Path," *Comm. ACM*, vol. 5, no. 6, p. 345, Jun. 1962.

48. J. D. Foley and A. Van Dam, *Fundamentals of Interactive Computer Graphics*, Addison-Wesley, 1982.

49. Y. Futamura, T. Kawai, H. Horikoshi, and M. Tsutsumi, "Development of Computer Programs by Problem Analysis Diagram (PAD)," *Proc. of 5th International*

Conf. on Software Engineering, 1981.

50.   E. R. Gansner, S. C. North, and K. P. Vo, "DAG - A Program that Draws Directed Graphs," *Software-Practice and Experience*, vol. 18, no. 11, pp. 1047-1062, Nov. 1988.

51.   M. R. Garey and D. S. Johnson, *Computers and Intractability: A Guide to the Theory of NP-Completeness*, Freeman, 1979.

52.   M. R. Garey and D. S. Johnson, "Crossing Number is NP-Complete," *SIAM J. Algebraic and Discrete Methods*, vol. 4, no. 3, pp. 312-316, 1983.

53.   A. Goldberg and D. Robson, *Smalltalk-80 The Language and its Implementation*, Addison-Wesley, 1983.

54.   J. Gosling, "Algebraic Constraints," Ph. D. dissertation, Dept. of Computer Science, Carnegie-Mellon Univ., Pittsburgh, 1983.

55.   R. B. Grafton and T. Ichikawa, "Visual Programming: Guest Editors' Introduction," *IEEE Computer*, vol. 18, no. 8, pp. 6-9, Aug. 1985.

56.   GSPC, "Status Report of the Graphics Standards Planning Committee," *Computer Graphics*, vol. 13, no. 3, Aug. 1979.

57.   A. C. Hearn, *REDUCE User's Manual, Version 3.3*, The Rand Corporation, Santa Monica, 1987.

58.   J. E. Hopcroft and R. E. Tarjan, "A V log V Algorithm for Isomorphism of Triconnected of Planar Graphs," *J. Comput. Syst. Sci.*, vol. 7, no. 3, pp. 323-331, Jun. 1973.

59.   E. L. Hutchins, J. D. Hollan, and D. A. Norman, "Direct Manipulation Interfaces," *Human-Computer Interaction*, vol. 1, pp. 311-338, 1985.

60.   R. J. K. Jacob, "A Specification Language for Direct-Manipulation User Interfaces," *ACM Trans. Graphics*, vol. 5, no. 4, pp. 283-317, Oct. 1986.

61.   S. C. Johnson, *YACC: Yet Another Compiler-Compiler*, UNIX Manual, vol. 2B, 1977.

62.   T. Kamada and S. Kawai, "An Enhanced Treatment of Hidden Lines," *ACM Trans. Graphics*, vol. 6, no. 4, pp. 308-323, Oct. 1987.

63.   T. Kamada and S. Kawai, "Interface for Visualizing Data: A Grammatical Approach (in Japanese)," *Graphics and CAD Rep. 30, Information Processing Society of Japan*, Nov. 1987.

64.   T. Kamada and S. Kawai, "Advanced Graphics for Visualization of Shielding Relations," *Computer Vision, Graphics, and Image Processing*, vol. 43, no. 3, pp. 294-312, Sep. 1988.

65.   T. Kamada and S. Kawai, "A Simple Method for Computing General Position in Displaying Three-dimensional Objects," *Computer Vision, Graphics, and Image Processing*, vol. 41, no. 1, pp. 43-56, Jan. 1988.

66.   T. Kamada and S. Kawai, "An Algorithm for Drawing General Undirected Graphs," *Information Processing Letters*, vol. 31, no. 1, pp. 7-15, Apr. 1989.

67.   S. E. Keene, *Object-Oriented Programming in COMMON LISP, A Programmer's Guide to CLOS*, Addison-Wesley, 1989.

68. B. W. Kernighan, "PIC - A Language for Typesetting Graphics," *Software-Practice and Experience*, vol. 12, no. 1, pp. 1-21, Jan. 1982.

69. B. W. Kernighan and L. L. Cherry, "A System for Typesetting Mathematics," *Comm. ACM*, vol. 18, no. 3, pp. 151-157, Mar. 1975.

70. D. E. Knuth, "Computer-Drawn Flowcharts," *Comm. ACM*, vol. 6, no. 9, pp. 555-563, Sep. 1963.

71. D. E. Knuth, "Semantics of Context-Free Languages," *Mathematical Systems Theory*, vol. 2, no. 2, pp. 127-145, 1968.

72. D. E. Knuth, *The Art of Computer Programming, Volume 1 Fundamental Algorithms*, Addison-Wesley, 1973.

73. D. E. Knuth, *TEX and METAFONT*, Digital Press, 1979.

74. M. Konopasek and S. Jayaraman, "Constraint and Declarative Languages for Engineering Applications: The TK!Solver Contribution," *Proceedings of the IEEE*, vol. 73, no. 12, pp. 1791-1806, Dec. 1985.

75. R. Kowalski, *Logic for Problem Solving*, Elsevier, 1979.

76. F. Lakin, "Spatial Parsing for Visual Languages," in *Visual Languages*, ed. S. K. Chang, pp. 35-85, Plenum Press, New York, 1986.

77. J. A. Larson, "Visual Languages for Database Users," in *Visual Languages*, ed. S. K. Chang, pp. 127-147, Plenum Press, New York, 1986.

78. C. Lassez, "Constraint Logic Programming," *BYTE*, vol. 12, no. 8, pp. 171-176, Aug. 1987.

79. W. Leler, "Constraint Languages for Computer-Aided Design," *ACM SIGDA Newsletter*, vol. 15, no. 2, pp. 11-15, 1985.

80. W. Leler, *Constraint Programming Languages, Their Specification and Generation*, Addison-Wesley, 1988.

81. R. J. Lipton, S. North, and J. Sandberg, "A Method for Drawing Graphs," *Proc. of the ACM Symposium on Computational Geometry*, no. 1985, pp. 153-160.

82. A. Lubiw, "Some NP-Complete Problems Similar to Graph Isomorphism," *SIAM J. Comput.*, vol. 10, no. 1, pp. 11-21, Feb. 1981.

83. J. Mackinlay, "Automating the Design of Graphical Presentations of Relational Information," *ACM Trans. Graphics*, vol. 5, no. 2, pp. 110-141, Apr. 1986.

84. MACSYMA Group, *MACSYMA Reference Manual, Version 10*, Symbolics Inc., 1984.

85. H. Maezawa, M. Kobayashi, K. Saito, and Y. Futamura, "Interactive System for Structured Program Production," *Proc. of 7th International Conf. on Software Engineering*, 1984.

86. E. Mäkinen, "On Circular Layouts," *Int. Journal of Computer Mathematics*, vol. 24, pp. 29-37, 1988.

87. J. Manning and M. J. Atallah, "Fast Detection and Display of Symmetry in Trees," Technical Rep. No. CSD-TR-562, Dept. of Computer Science, Purdue Univ., West Lafayette, Dec. 1985.

88. J. Manning and M. J. Atallah, "Fast Detection and Display of Symmetry in Outer-planar Graphs," Technical Rep. No. CSD-TR-606, Dept. of Computer Science, Purdue Univ., West Lafayette, Jun. 1986.

89. J. M. Mata, "Solving Systems of Linear Equalities and Inequalities Efficiently," *Proc. of 15th Southeastern Conf. on Combinatorics, Graph Theory and Computing*, pp. 251-260, Mar. 1984.

90. J. M. Mata, "ALLENDE: A Procedural Language for the Hierarchical Specification of VLSI Layouts," *Proc. of the ACM IEEE 22nd Design Automation Conf.*, pp. 183-189, 1985.

91. B. H. McCormick, T. A. DeFanti, and M. D. Brown, "Visualization in Scientific Computing," *Computer Graphics*, vol. 21, no. 6, Nov. 1987.

92. E. B. Messinger, "Automatic Layout of Large Directed Graphs," Technical Rep. No. 88-07-08, Dept. of Computer Science, Univ. of Washington, Seattle, Jul. 1988.

93. H. B. Mittal, "A Fast Backtrack Algorithm for Graph Isomorphism," *Information Processing Letters*, vol. 29, no. 2, pp. 105-110, Sep. 1988.

94. A. Moffat and T. Takaoka, "An All Pairs Shortest Path Algorithm with Expected Running Time $O(n^2 \log n)$," *Proc. of 26th Annual Symposium on Foundations of Computer Science*, pp. 101-105, Oct. 1985.

95. B. A. Myers, "INCENSE: A System for Displaying Data Structures," *Computer Graphics*, vol. 17, no. 3, pp. 115-125, Jul. 1983.

96. B. A. Myers, *Creating User Interfaces by Demonstration*, Academic Press, Boston, 1988.

97. I. Nassi and B. Shneiderman, "Flowchart Techniques for Structured· Programming," *ACM SIGPLAN Notices*, vol. 8, no. 8, pp. 12-26, Aug. 1973.

98. G. Nelson, "Juno, A Constraint-Based Graphics System," *Computer Graphics*, vol. 19, no. 3, pp. 235-243, Jul. 1985.

99. T. Pavlidis and C. J. Van Wyk, "An Automatic Beautifier for Drawings and Illustrations," *Computer Graphics*, vol. 19, no. 3, pp. 225-234, Jul. 1985.

100. L. A. Pineda, "A Compositional Semantics for Graphics," *Proc. of Eurographics '88, Elsevier Science Publisher B.V.*, 1988.

101. L. A. Pineda and N. Chater, "GRAFLOG: Programming with Interactive Graphics and PROLOG," *Proc. of CG International '88, Springer-Verlag*, pp. 469-478, 1988.

102. L. A. Pineda, E. Klein, and J. Lee, "GRAFLOG: Understanding Drawings through Natural Language," *Computer Graphics Forum*, vol. 7, no. 2, pp. 97-103, Jun. 1988.

103. M. C. Pong and N. Ng, "PIGS - A System for Programming with Interactive Graphical Support," *Software-Practice and Experience*, vol. 13, no. 9, pp. 847-855, Sep. 1983.

104. F. P. Preparata and M. I. Shamos, *Computational Geometry, An Introduction* Springer-Verlag, New York, 1985.

105. N. R. Quinn and M. A. Breuer, "A Forced Directed Component Placement Procedure for Printed Circuit Boards," *IEEE Trans. Circuits and Systems*, vol. CAS-26, no. 6, pp. 377-388, Jun. 1979.

106. G. Raeder, "A Survey of Current Graphical Programming Techniques," *IEEE Computer*, vol. 18, no. 8, pp. 11-25, Aug. 1985.

107. C. R. Rao, *Linear Statistical Inference and Its Applications, 2nd Ed.*, John Wiley & Sons, 1973.

108 M. G. Reggiani and F. E. Marchetti, "A Proposed Method for Representing Hierarchies," *IEEE Trans. Syst., Man, Cybern.*, vol. SMC-18, no. 1, pp. 2-8, Jan./Feb. 1988.

109. E. M. Reingold and J. S. Tilford, "Tider Drawings of Trees," *IEEE Trans. Software Eng.*, vol. SE-7, no. 2, pp. 223-228, Mar. 1981.

110. E. Rich, *Artificial Intelligence*, McGraw-Hill, 1983.

111. J. A. Roach, "The Rectangle Placement Language," *Proc. of the ACM IEEE 21st Design Automation Conf.*, pp. 405-411, Jun. 1984.

112. L. A. Rowe, M. Davis, E. Messinger, C. Meyer, C. Spirakis, and A. Tuan, "A Browser for Directed Graphs," *Software-Practice and Experience*, vol. 17, no. 1, pp. 61-76, Jan. 1987.

113. K. Sakai and A. Aiba, "CAL: A Theoretical Background of Constraint Logic Programming and its Applications," Technical Rep. No. 364, ICOT Research Center, Tokyo, Japan, Apr. 1988.

114. R. Sedgewick, *Algorithms*, Addison-Wesley, Massachusetts, 1983.

115. T. Shimomura, "A Method for Automatically Generating Business Graphs," *IEEE Computer Graphics and Applications*, vol. 3, no. 6, pp. 55-59, Sep. 1983.

116. B. Shneiderman, "Direct Manipulation: A Step Beyond Programming Languages," *IEEE Computer*, vol. 16, no. 8, pp. 57-69, Aug. 1983.

117. B. Shneiderman, *Designing the User Interface: Strategies for Effective Human-Computer Interaction*, Addison-Wesley, 1987.

118. B. Shneiderman, R. Mayer, D. Mckay, and P. Heller, "Experimental Investigation of the Utility of Detailed Flowcharts in Programming," *Comm. ACM*, vol. 20, no. 6, pp. 373-381, Jun. 1977.

119. N. C. Shu, "Visual Programming Languages: A Perspective and a Dimensional Analysis," in *Visual Languages*, ed. S. K. Chang, pp. 11-34, Plenum Press, New York, 1986.

120. J. Slocum, "A Survey of Machine Translation: Its History, Current Status, and Future Prospects," *Computational Linguistics*, vol. 11, no. 1, pp. 1-17, Jan./Mar. 1985.

121. P. M. Spira, "A New Algorithm for Finding All Shortest Paths in a Graph of Positive Arcs in Average Time $O(n^2\log^2 n)$," *SIAM J. Comput.*, vol. 2, no. 1, pp. 28-32, Mar. 1973.

122. K. Sugiyama, "Achieving Uniqueness Requirement in Drawing Digraphs: Optimum Code Algorithm and Hierarchy Isomorphism," Research Rep. No. 58, IIAS-SIS, FUJITSU, Japan, 1985.

123. K. Sugiyama and K. Misue, "Visualizing Structural Information: Hierarchical Drawing of a Compound Digraph," Research Rep. No. 86, IIAS-SIS, FUJITSU, Japan, 1989.

124. K. Sugiyama, S. Tagawa, and M. Toda, "Methods for Visual Understanding of Hierarchical System Structures," *IEEE Trans. Syst., Man, Cybern.*, vol. SMC-11, no. 2, pp. 109-125, Feb. 1981.

125. G. J. Sussman and G. L. Steele, "CONSTRAINTS - A Language for Expressing Almost-Hierarchical Descriptions," *Artificial Intelligence*, vol. 14, no. 1, pp. 1-39, Jan. 1980.

126. I. E. Sutherland, "Sketchpad: A Man-Machine Graphical Communication System," *Proc. of Spring Joint Computer Conf.*, pp. 329-346, 1963.

127. P. A. Szekely and B. A. Myers, "A User Interface Toolkit Based on Graphical Objects and Constraints," *Proc. of OOPSLA '88*, pp. 36-45, San Diego, Sep. 1988.

128. R. Tamassia, C. Batini, and M. Talamo, "An Algorithm for Automatic Layout of Entity Relationship Diagrams," in *Entity-Relationship Approach to Software Engineering*, ed. R. Yeh, pp. 421-439, Elsevier Science Publisher B.V., Amsterdam, North-Holland, 1983.

129. R. Tamassia, G. Battista, and C. Batini, "Automatic Graph Drawing and Readability of Diagrams," *IEEE Trans. Syst., Man, Cybern.*, vol. SMC-18, no. 1, pp. 61-79, Jan./Feb. 1988.

130. P. J. W. Ten Hagen, "ILP Intermediate Language for Pictures," Mathematical Center Tracts 130, Amsterdam, 1980.

131. D. Thalmann, "An Interactive Data Visualization System," *Software-Practice and Experience*, vol. 14, no. 3, pp. 277-290, Mar. 1984.

132. J. F. Traub, *Iterative Methods for the Solution of Equations*, Prentice-Hall, Englewood Cliffs, N.J., 1964.

133. D. C. Tsichritzis and F. H. Lochovsky, *Data Base Management Systems*, Academic Press, New York, 1977.

134. W. T. Tutte, "How to Draw a Graph," *Proc. of the London Mathematical Society*, vol. 3, no. 13, pp. 743-768, 1963.

135. J. D. Ullman, *Principles of Database Systems*, Computer Science Press, 1982.

136. J. D. Ullman, *Computational Aspects of VLSI*, Computer Science Press, 1984.

137. C. J. Van Wyk, "A High-Level Language for Specifying Pictures," *ACM Trans. Graphics*, vol. 1, no. 2, pp. 163-182, Apr. 1982.

138. B. T. Vander Zanden, "Constraint Grammars in User Interface Management Systems," *Proc. of Graphics Interface '88*, pp. 176-184, Edmonton, Jun. 1988.

139. J. G. Vaucher, "Pretty-Printing of Trees," *Software-Practice and Experience*, vol. 10, no. 7, pp. 553-561, Jul. 1980.

140. J. N. Warfield, "Crossing Theory and Hierarchy Mapping," *IEEE Trans. Syst., Man, Cybern.*, vol. SMC-7, no. 7, pp. 505-523, Jul. 1977.

141. H. Watanabe, "Heuristic Graph Displayer for G-BASE," Technical Rep. No. 5, Ricoh Software Research Center, Tokyo, Japan, Aug. 1987.

142. C. Wetherell and A. Shannon, "Tidy Drawings of Trees," *IEEE Trans. Software Eng.*, vol. SE-5, no. 5, pp. 514-520, Sep. 1979.

143. R. M. White, "Applying Direct Manipulation to Geometric Construction Systems," *Proc. of CG International '88, Springer-Verlag*, pp. 446-455, 1988.

144. T. Winograd, *Language as a Cognitive Process,* Addison-Wesley, 1983.

145. F. Zdybel, N. R. Greenfeld, M. D. Yonke, and J. Gibbons, "An Information Presentation System," *Proc. of IJCAI '81*, pp. 978-984, Aug. 1981.

INDEX